International Design Yearbook
14

International Design Yearbook
14

Editor – Jasper Morrison
General Editor – Michael Horsham
Assistant Editor – Jennifer Hudson
Art Direction/Design – Tomato

Abbeville Press Publishers
New York London Paris

First published in the United States of America in 1999
by Abbeville Press, 22 Cortlandt Street, New York, NY 10007

First published in Great Britain in 1999 by Laurence King Publishing
an imprint of Calmann & King Ltd
71 Great Russell Street
London WC1B 3BN
e-mail – enquiries@Calmann-King.co.uk

Copyright © 1999 Calmann & King Ltd

All rights reserved. No part of this publication may be reproduced or transmitted in any form or by any means, electronic or mechanical, including photocopy, recording or any information storage and retrieval system, without permission in writing from the publisher.

ISBN 0-7892-0511-4

First edition
10 9 8 7 6 5 4 3 2 1

Based on an original idea by Stuart Durant
Printed in Hong Kong

International Design Yearbook
14

Contents

Introductions	002–013
Furniture	014–075
Lighting	076–103
Tableware	104–141
Textiles	142–169
Products	170–219
Biographies	220–227
Acquisitions	228–230
Photographic Credits	231
Suppliers	232

Introductions

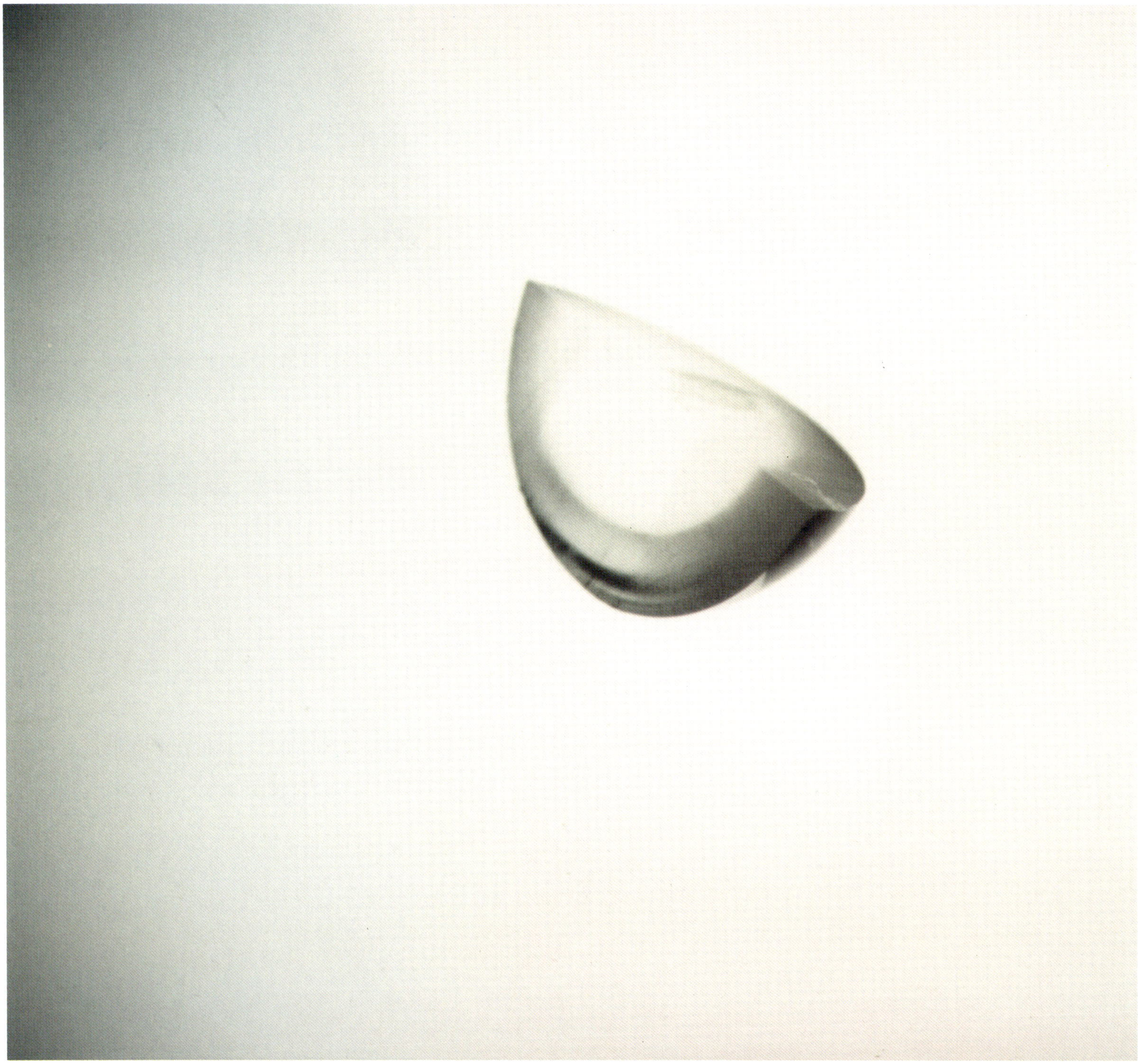

As Buckminster Fuller once explained, design can be defined as a process giving order to a set of components in such a way as to fulfil a purpose or a function. Today that definition, while succinct, seems not to cover the whole story. A product that doesn't work will not get produced, and yet good function alone is no guarantee of success for a product. Designers must give visual and conceptual order to an object, and at the same time provide something harder to define: 'objectality'. Nowadays even a power drill needs good objectality. Objectality is a bit like built-in advertising, it sends out a subliminal (or not so subliminal) message to prospective customers. Different objectalities attract and repel different people for different reasons, but without an objectality which appeals to a wide enough audience, a product will not succeed. As with movies, the best-selling products are not always the most interesting. Designers have to balance commercial awareness with academic interests and moral beliefs and come up with products that satisfy their own standards.

In the 1920s it was the development of tubular steel processes and composite wood materials that led to design innovation. The 1990s have seen enormous growth in plastic technology. The sophistication of the technology has given designers greater freedom and possibilities and at the same time has led to greater dependence on the engineer. Plastic is no longer the environmental bogeyman it once was. New ways of calculating net energy costs over the full life-cycle of a product show plastic high on the list of cleaner materials. The future is gas-injected plastic mouldings, combination moulding of plastics which perform separate functions, aerated aluminium pressure moulding, super-formed aluminium sheet and laminated wood mouldings which can be robot-cut into component form. The emphasis is on achieving greater performance from materials and processing them more efficiently. The armoury of new processes (and there are many more than those mentioned) presents designers with a richer palette of possibility than ever before.

Introductions – Jasper Morrison

Since the mid-eighties drawing boards have been replaced by computers; ships curves and compasses by sophisticated drawing software; post-office deliveries by fax and more recently e-mail and ISDN. All this, combined with technological developments, explains the increasing sophistication of products and the speed of change. It's not unusual for a design studio to ISDN three-dimensional drawings of a product to a European sister of a multi-national model-making company, and for the finished model to be couriered back from Osaka in three or four days, just because there was spare capacity on the CNC machines there. Eventually designers will have their own stereo lithography equipment, allowing models to be run off in the studio, as prints of drawings are now. European industry has developed an appetite for and an understanding of design, which is resulting in more and more diverse clients and work. The specialized areas of design study in European schools have become increasingly inadequate as training for the wider range of products that a designer can expect to deal with in the real world. Design is after all a process of getting more out of products either aesthetically, functionally or commercially, and there is no reason why a designer who can design chairs or sofas should not design a TV or a car.

Can individual creativity keep up with this pace and has the creative process changed? Yes and no, not very much. Designing a wider range of products at any given time can be more creatively stimulating than doing fewer, as each project feeds the other. The starting point for any design still depends on a moment of inspiration which is just as hard to predict, plan or quantify as it ever was. There is no textbook approach to a design problem, solutions are always arrived at in unexpected ways. What has changed is that this is more of an accepted fact than it used to be. Design schools used to preach that design problems could only be solved by rational analysis of functional requirements and practical application of appropriate technology. This dry and uninspiring model was responsible for the cul-de-sac in which design found itself in the early 1980s. Memphis blew away these rules and simultaneously ushered in a period of postmodern confusion during which designers forgot that they were designing for people and started designing directly for museum pedestals, as if the system had short-circuited. The vacuum of responsibility towards the consumer combined with the lack of rules brought about a revival of creativity in design and a reappraisal of modernism.

It isn't hard to see with hindsight that the missing ingredient which led to modernism's temporary downfall was humour, or at least a lightness of touch, which took into account that while a product was born to industry, it was destined to spend the rest of its life with people, who might not be interested in the dry logic of manufacturing solutions. The flip side was a return to modernist principles without any of the constraints which had made it so tedious to the consumer. Looking back there was nothing wrong with modernism, it just needed an oil change. It might be true to say that modernism was simply the name given to mankind's reaction to the possibilities that the machine age presented. We tend to get tired of names and maybe wrongly conclude that what they represent must also be exhausted. If we think of modernism as a method rather than a movement it's easier to conclude that it's a method which is perfectly capable of adapting with the times to provide what's needed. It's a fact that the physical appearance of an object is to most people most of that object's presence, but perhaps too much importance is attached to it. If we thought form less important we might develop a sensibility for other qualities in an object. Designing in a way that allows other aspects of an object's make-up to propose its form may be a step in the right direction.

The recent explosion of young design talent in Europe and the injection of new ideas exhibit modernist tendencies which are fresh. The best of them contain a conceptual element which makes use of forms borrowed or adapted from different applications, and a subtle play with materials which, combined with the right emphasis, bring new and interesting results. If they collectively appear to ape fashion (in the sense that a definite style exists, which sometimes outweighs content) it could be explained by the fact that here is a generation which is completely in tune with itself and its moment both socially and philosophically. Let's not forget either that the younger a designer is, the less access to and experience of technology and industry they have, and that without this the available processes and materials are by nature restricted to a narrow range of practical alternatives.

Shedding the constraints of an old design order has made for much freer and more open sources of inspiration for designers, and this in turn has meant that every product has been up for reappraisal, even the humble toilet brush. The consumer market which used to be a dirty word in design circles has responded well to designers' renewed interest in it and has reinforced industry's need of design. We are in a period of flux as we approach the new millennium, it only remains for the more conservative (industrial) end of product design to accept this new freedom.

Jasper Morrison

Door Handle – Series 1144
anodized aluminium
FSB – Germany – 1990

Sofa System – Orly
stainless steel – upholstery
h 73cm – w 80–260cm – d 80cm
h 28¾in – w 31½–102⅜in – d 31½in
Cappellini – Italy – 1998

Introductions – Jasper Morrison

File Holder – X-X
aluminium – PP
h 26cm – w 38cm – d 34cm
h 10½in – w 15in – d 13⅜in
Magis – Italy – 1998

Table System – Atlas
spun steel – aluminium – laminate
Alias – Italy – 1992

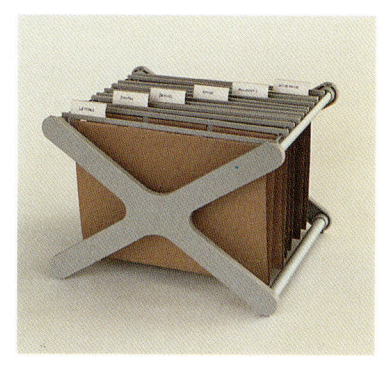

Ply Chair
plywood
h 84cm – w 40cm – d 40cm
h 33in – w 15¾in – d 15¾in
Vitra – Germany – 1988

Kitchen Boxes – Tin Family
stainless steel
h 8–13cm – di 10–28cm
h 3 1/8–5 1/8in – di 4–11in
Alessi – Italy – 1998

Suspension Light – Glo-ball
opalescent glass
150w E27 bulb
di 45cm
di 17 3/4in
Flos – Italy – 1998

Pepper and Salt Mills – Pepe le Moko
PA – stainless steel
h 12cm – di 7cm
h 4 3/4in – di 2 3/4in
Alessi – Italy – 1998

Tray-Table – Op-la
ABS – stainless steel
h 52cm – di 48cm
h 20 1/2in – di 18 7/8in
Alessi – Italy – 1998

Introductions – Jasper Morrison

Jasper Morrison and John Tree
(Sony Design Centre Europe)
Flat-screen Television
1998

Jasper Morrison and John Tree
(Sony Design Centre Europe)
Hi-fi System
1998

The process of putting together the *International Design Yearbook* has proved once again to be an intriguing one. Having resolved two years ago to move the book forward in terms of its content and the way that content is presented, we again found ourselves deluged with images from which a contemporary survey of design had to be forged. The main problem, as ever, was finding a theme with which to discuss the content. With such a wide range of approaches to the problems of design, the likelihood of finding a set of ideas which could bind the selection together was low. With the involvement of Jasper Morrison, however, the likelihood of an assiduous and reasoned selection was high. Between those two poles the book would come into being.

As expected, the final selection is formally and materially diverse. We encompass new fabrics as well as new formulations of design staples — bicycles, cutlery and vessels. It would be a mistake to over-subscribe to the idea that commonality can be found in such a selection of objects. After all, these are images of work that have come into prototype or production for a variety of reasons, inventive and economic. These objects are designed to serve different purposes, fill exceedingly different gaps in the market, solve functional problems or to allow the designer to further explore a personal project.

In terms of the thematic content of the book, therefore, I have had to look for a theme which is intellectually abstract. It's a truism that the definition of the role of the designer in the twentieth century is closely allied to the definition and discussion of the idea of the object, and equally that objects have the capacity to transmit and carry meanings above and beyond their everyday function. In fact, the only common link amongst the objects on display here is their status as objects, as things invented and designed by women and men. So what to make of all of this stuff?

Introductions – Michael Horsham

Now in the late twentieth century we are perhaps feeling the absence of a coherent programmatic and socially responsible initiative in design. The vagaries of the market place have ensured that the drive amongst designers is generally to produce objects which sell and which, at times, pander to the whims of fashion and marketing. This was not always the case. The modes of making and selling, of designing things for the home, have had other agendas thrust upon them by history but also by contemporary economic, social and philosophical circumstance.

At the end of the last century, as Europe's leading industrialized nation, Germany gave birth to a number of ideas and methodologies which are with us today. Throughout the nineteenth century Germany had come to prominence as an industrial power through some seemingly collective desire to master iterative processes. The chemical, steel and electrical industries which underpinned Germany's growth were predicated on the ability to control and understand operations to the degree that could be repeated *ad infinitum* with little or no deviation in terms of the quality of the result. To Germans (and more generally Europeans) involved in the businesses of design, engineering and manufacture in the run up to the end of the last century, the idea of certainty in the end results of design and manufacture became increasingly key. The change in Germany's fortunes saw political unification succeeded by seismic changes in the nature of the relationship to the land itself. Germany changed along with other European states from being largely an agrarian economy to an industrial economy. This rapid urbanization and industrialization meant that, in the minds of conservative thinkers, the 'real nature' of Germany was being forsaken for the onward march of progress and modernity. In a simplistic scheme, the machine-made belonged to the new world of standard practice, the handworked belonged to the old world of romantic ideas and history.

The value of the handworked over that which was produced by machine – and the debates over their relative merits which ensued in the early years of the twentieth century – seemed to characterize the philosophical split between mind and body, hand and heart, the romantic, artistic soul of the nation and its burgeoning industrial base. The discussions within the Deutscher Werkbund, principally between Henri Van de Velde and Hermann Muthesius from 1907 onwards concerning the conflict between craftsmanship and standardization dominated the proceedings of that organization through the early years of the century, but in many ways, to coin a phrase, the die had been cast for Germany and by extension, mass production and the future of the industrially-produced object in Europe.

In Europe and worldwide there were other examples of the march of progress. In France, Art Nouveau at the hands of Hector Guimard in particular, became a modular system for modern production. In Great Britain, the manufacture of railways and ships had long been the home of standardized engineering and production techniques. For a short time Belgium was the centre of tramway and electrical motor production. In America, the meat packers of Chicago had famously standardized the production line in the mid-nineteenth century, Taylorism had taken hold of the philosophy of production, and by the first decade of the new century Henry Ford was producing (albeit hand-finished) cars from a production line. In Japan what is now the mighty Matsushita Corporation was founded in 1918. All of these operations depended upon the development of systems of mass production – all depended upon the idea of the object as a machine – rather than hand-produced artefact. It was in Germany, however, that the cultural effects of the ideas of objectivity, standardization and serial production were first analysed and put into practice on a social scale and with social intent. Ultimately, the calls for the standardization of the infrastructure of production, from screws to paper sizes, from bolts to steel gauges, meant that the 'workmanship of risk' which characterizes all proto-industrial manufacturing economies could effectively be eliminated from the motor which was driving Germany's ascension into the upper echelons of the industrial world from which it has yet to descend.

The workmanship of risk is in itself an interesting idea which deserves some comment here. The phrase was coined by the craftsman David Pye to distinguish between those objects that are made by hand with a degree of skill which, if abandoned even for a moment, would result in the object's failure, and those objects that are made using industrial and mass-produced techniques. The workmanship of risk is anathema to the object designed for serial production. Products in the latter category reap the economies of scale afforded by the manufacture of components and objects which are guaranteed to drop off the end of the production line in a more or less perfect state. The workmanship of certainty is the holy grail towards which the developed world has apparently been striving. Perhaps because German industrial processes were advanced early on in the century and perhaps because the well-being of the nation depended upon that advancement, the idea of the dispassionate analysis of the object in terms of its form and function changed from being that which concerned the engineers to that which concerned the designers, the architects and the theoreticians. By 1909, Peter Behrens had embarked on the corporate design programme of the Allgemeine Elektrizitäts-Gesellschaft (AEG), a process which demanded an at times dispassionate objectification of not only the processes of manufacture but the inherent quality of the things that were ultimately produced. By 1927 the Deutscher Werkbund was behind the Weissenhof Siedlung: a development of houses and flats in a suburb of Stuttgart which resolutely pursued at least the formal languages if not the production methods of modern housing. The Frankfurt Kitchen – designed by Grete Schütte-Lihotsky in 1924, the concept of *Existenz minimum* discussed by architects at various CIAM meetings in the inter-war years, and the increasing cultural currency of the idea of modernity also added to the progress of the 'objectification of objects'. The understanding that things could be stripped of their historical associations in order to reveal their functional presence, and that that very same functional presence could contribute to the generation of formal languages and codes that owed little to

Introductions – Michael Horsham

traditional modes of decoration and yet still be beautiful, useful and therefore socially enriching, was the result of the experiments in a new-found interest in objectivity – new objectivity or 'neue Sachlichkeit'.

Such is the German language, with its facility for compounding words and concepts, that it has an ideal term to describe qualities of objects and approaches to the design of things. 'Sachlichkeit' is the German word for objectivity. As translation exposes the foreignness of languages, so the use of the word Sachlichkeit hints at a depth of meaning and an appropriateness to the idea of objectivity *vis à vis* design which in this case leaves humble English far behind.

The German word for 'a thing' is Sache (f.); the word as part of Sachlichkeit pertains to the idea of the thing, the quality of the object. A close approximation of the depth hinted at by the term might be 'thingness' or closer still, 'thinglyness'. Clearly, such a word is clumsy in English but it serves to highlight the paucity of ways in which some languages can describe our own relationships to things. Nevertheless, the essence of the things we own, and which are designed, the drive to find, discuss and name the qualitative essence of things constitutes the building blocks of a philosophical conundrum within which we are asked to name and articulate our feelings as they relate to the mute world of objects. Sachlichkeit, and the 'neue Sachlichkeit' were, then, key terms in the raft of ideas which fuelled the rise of modernism and its relationship to industrial processes. The language which grew up to describe the manufacture of things and the relationship of the designer to the thing designed reflected the somewhat mythologized change in the role of the formgiver from artisan or artist to designer. In truth, many of the formal languages and exemplars of modernism and 'new objectivity' were as reliant on so-called craft skills as objects for the home had ever been. Many new things were still made using old skills and not new machines. But if it was not on craft skills, then it was certainly on the home that the new objectivity was centred.

Today we have evidence in the shape of this book that the driving force of objectivity in the design process has persevered. But we also have evidence that other forces are at work on the design of goods for the home. This is as it should be, for if objects were to be conceived with only an objective analysis of their function and form at their core then they would speak less of their time and the people who were involved in their generation. So, in the field of goods designed for serial production, it is still possible to find reworkings of traditional materials and forms. It is still possible to find work that has been made or finished by hand, and although this strand of craftsman-like skills applied to objects does not equate significantly to the 'workmanship of risk' there are human marks and the signifiers of human values built into the machine-made world. At best this is what designers do: they take the idea of the human and meld it with the abstract, objective idea of the object. We stand at the end of a century in which our attitudes to the design and manufacture of goods for the home have been radically reshaped by our fascination with machines and modernity, with the mythology of objectivity. The results of that synthesis, as the contents of this book show, cannot help but be many and varied, with varying degrees of success. This is, of course, exactly as it should be.

Michael Horsham

Furniture

Furniture design revolves around staples – chairs, sofas, tables and storage – and the task of the furniture designer is often to re-invent elements of these categories which, frankly, do not need re-invention. The market and the culture, however, tell us otherwise. The market for modern furniture continues to expand beyond Italy, its traditional home. This means that there is new space being found for new forms and new formal languages, even though many of the functions performed by furniture-types are destined never to change. The culture, on the other hand, thrives upon the idea of design and the idea of the new. In short, the market wants 'more', and the culture wants 'new'. Together these forces create the circumstances within which, occasionally, designers are able to elide forms and functions which were previously distinct in order to create a truly new object for the home. Marry those opportunities with continuing progress in material technology and the continuing cultural focus on the home and furniture design will continue to concern the re-invention of typical forms. Within that process of re-invention, though, a significant part of pure invention should subsist.

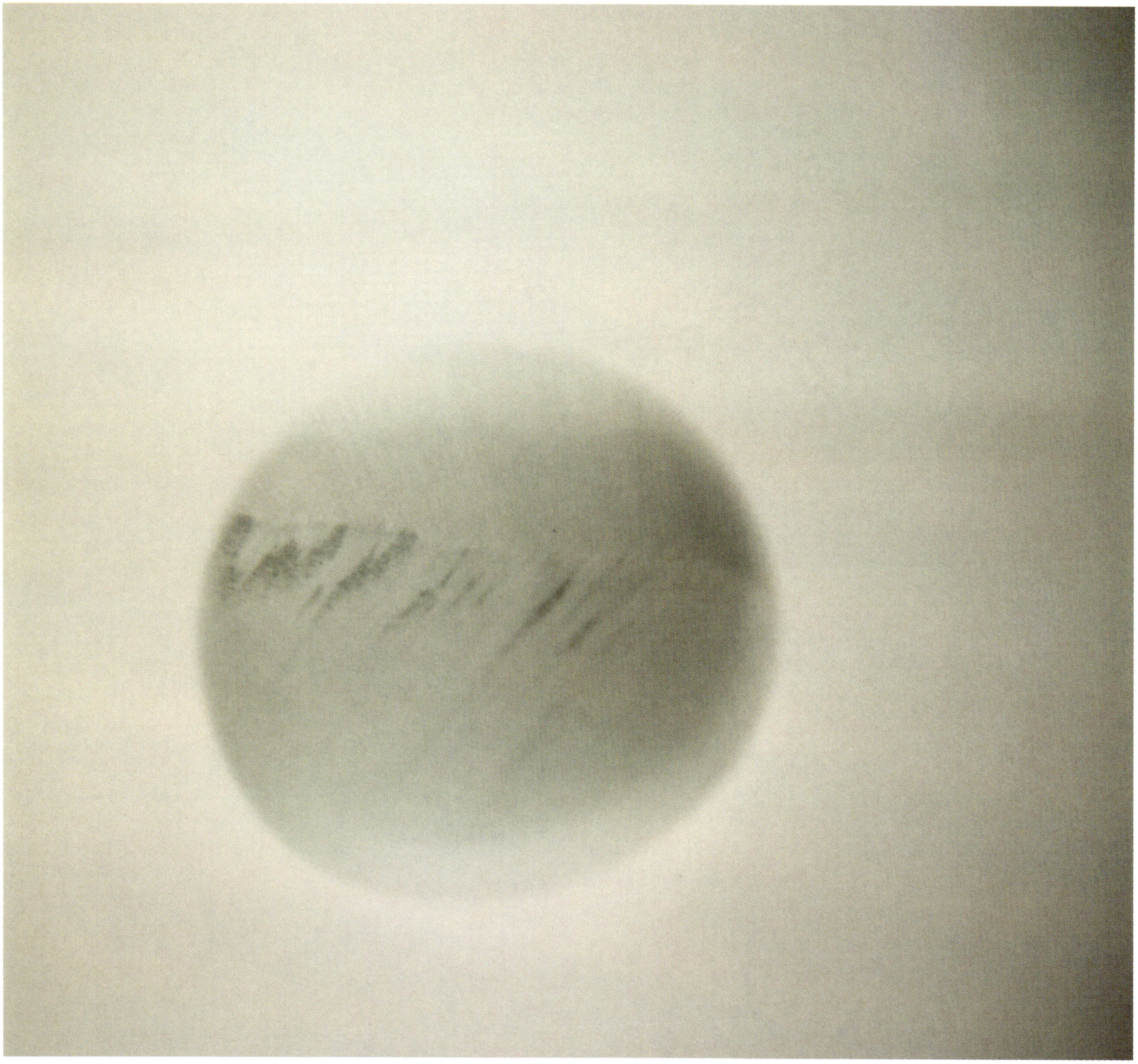

James Irvine
Sofa-bed – Lunar
aluminium – painted steel – polyurethane
sofa – h 72cm – w 225cm – d 80cm
       h 28 3/8in – w 88 5/8in – d 31 1/2in
bed – h 40cm – w 225cm – d 131cm
      h 15 3/4in – w 88 5/8in – d 51 5/8in
B & B Italia – Italy

Coffee Table – Lunar
wood – aluminium
h 52.5cm – di 38cm
h 20 5/8in – di 15in
B & B Italia – Italy

Furniture

François Bauchet
Chair – Chauffeuse Meridienne
wood – upholstery
h 53cm – w 110cm – d 60cm
h 20⁷⁄₈in – w 43¹⁄₄in – d 23⁵⁄₈in
Néotù – France

Spatial needs are continually changing and with changing needs come changing forms of furniture. The idea of comfortable furniture which can be reconfigured grew from the philosophies of minimum existence and the maximum utilization of minimum space. Hence, particularly in the post-war era when newly built dwellings would boast rooms which had to have more than one use, sofas which could be transformed into beds became commonplace. The two pieces of furniture here answer different needs in terms of reconfiguration. James Irvine's sofa-bed is a fresh reworking of a familiar Italian theme. The coupling of coffee tables with the sofa-bed reconfigures the tables by default: as the sofa converts its form, so the coffee tables convert their use. Bauchet's chair is designed to reconfigure for comfort and not for the demands of multiple use and utility. – MH

Rock Galpin
Sofa – Aeron
ply laminate – steel
h 85cm – w 123cm – d 80cm
h 33½in – w 48⅜in – d 31½in
Studio Orange – UK

Furniture

Andrew Stafford
Sofa – Stafford
moulded GRP – American oak – multi-density foam
h 80cm – w 217cm – d 87cm
h 31½in – w 85⅜in – d 34½in
SCP – UK

Furniture design, when it is doing its prescribed job, not only introduces new forms, but also generates new combinations of materials. Where new formal languages and surprising mixtures of materials coincide there is usually a piece of furniture which is worth commenting upon. Andrew Stafford's sofa for SCP is one such piece. The moulded form of the GRP 'bucket' which constitutes the main structural element of the piece uses a material which is renowned for its resilience and plasticity. The forging of a unified piece from traditional upholstery and modern material is admittedly difficult, but this sofa's formal strength relies on the smooth transitions between materials. These transitions are helped along by the family of geometric forms which bind the otherwise disparate elements and materials together. Rock Galpin's sofa is also a distinctive and playful combination of materials, in this case, steel, upholstery and plywood, but the distinctions between the materials are highlighted through colour and proximity. – MH

Roberto Barbieri
Sofa – Olimpo
steel – polyurethane – dacron
h 78cm – w 216cm – d 85cm
h 30¾in – w 85in – d 33½in
Zanotta – Italy

Furniture

Antonio Citterio
Sofa – Theo
metal – polyurethane – chromed aluminium
h 78cm – w 260cm – d 98cm
h 30¾in – w 102⅜in – d 38⅝in
Flexform – Italy

Patricia Urquiola
Sofa – Step
metal – upholstery
h 76cm – w 220cm – d 102cm
h 29⅞in – w 86⅝in – d 42½in
Moroso – Italy

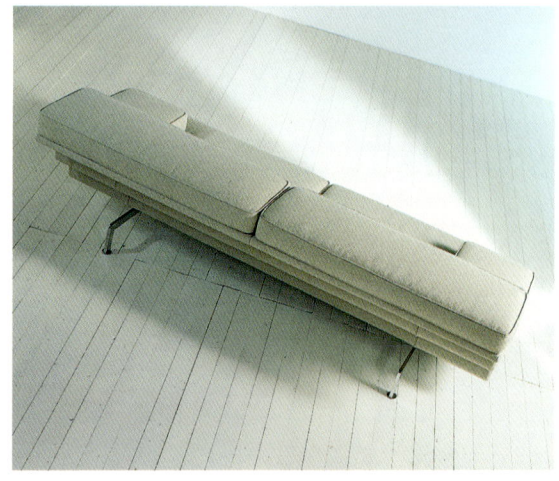

Furniture

Vico Magistretti
Sofa – Palestro
steel – polyurethane – anodized aluminium
h 71cm – w 235cm – d 90cm
h 28in – w 92½in – d 35½in
De Padova – Italy

Massimo Iosa Ghini
Sofa – Hi-Pop
steel – polyurethane – polyester fibre – cherrywood – aluminium
h 78cm – w 240cm – d 96cm
h 30¾in – w 94½in – d 37¾in
Moroso – Italy

Sigla (Marina Bani – Patrizia Scarzella – Marco Penati)
Sofa – Nadir
steel – polyurethane – dacron
h 80cm – w 120cm/153cm/230cm – d 79cm/82cm/120cm
h 31½in – w 47½in/60¼in/90⅝in – d 31⅛in/32¼in/47½in
Zanotta – Italy

Furniture

Antonio Citterio
Sofa – Charles
die-cast aluminium – upholstery
h 86cm – w 228cm – d 95cm
h 33 ⅞in – w 89¾in – d 37⅜in
B. & B Italia – Italy

The arrangement of furniture into seating groups comes from a tradition of design which looked to create a new flexibility in interior organization. The notion that the modern home was the locus of social activity, and not simply the place where people returned from work for shelter and sustenance, shaped the way in which designers could think about staple furniture forms. Thus the sofa mutates into the L-form group. Significantly, the designs on these pages are from Italy – arguably the country which has done most in the last thirty years to redefine the forms of modern domestic furniture. – MH

Tom Dixon
Chaise – Hoop
tubular stainless steel – beech
h 66cm – w 206cm – d 66cm
h 26in – w 81⅛in – d 26in
SCP – UK

Furniture

Marcel Wanders
Carpet/chaise – Nomad
wool
w 200cm – d 80cm/200cm
w 78¾in – d 31½in/78¾in
Cappellini – Italy

Furniture continues to mutate for any number of reasons. On this page, Marcel Wanders pursues his exploration and expropriation of forms. By placing the familiar in unfamiliar settings, or devising seemingly inappropriate uses for staples, the lexicon of forms is forced to move on. On the other hand, Tom Dixon's piece is clearly a move to establish a strand of design which is demonstrably different from what has gone before – in personal terms at least. – MH

028

Alfredo Häberli and Christophe Marchand
Chaise – Matrable
wood – iron – foam rubber
h 85cm – w 280cm – d 100cm
h 33 1/2in – w 110 1/4in – d 39 3/8in
Bourse VIA – France
prototype

The capacity for reconfiguration is a corollary of technique and technology. This sofa offers the potential for a number of configurations, none of which disrupt or disfigure the already quirky geometry. Its status as a prototype means that pushing the idea of flexibility this far may not find its way into the homes of many people. The existence of such pieces as ideas is nevertheless important. Whether such a piece goes into production or not, its very existence allows for the possibility of change and development in terms of the formal languages of traditional pieces of furniture. – MH

Furniture

Björn Dahlström
Bench Seat – Bank
polyurethane – cotton – metal
h 65cm – w 200cm – d 45cm
h 25¾in – w 78¾in – d 17¾in
Zoltan – Italy

Gioia Meller Marcovicz
Garden Furniture – Dia
stainless steel – water-repellent fabrics – laminate
chaise – h 30cm – w 192cm – d 64cm
    h 11¾in – w 75⅝in – d 25⅛in
chair – h 88cm – w 48cm – d 77cm
    h 34⅝in – w 18⅞in – d 30⅜in
table – h 71cm – w 152cm – d 85cm
    h 28in – w 59⅞in – d 33½in
ClassiCon – Germany

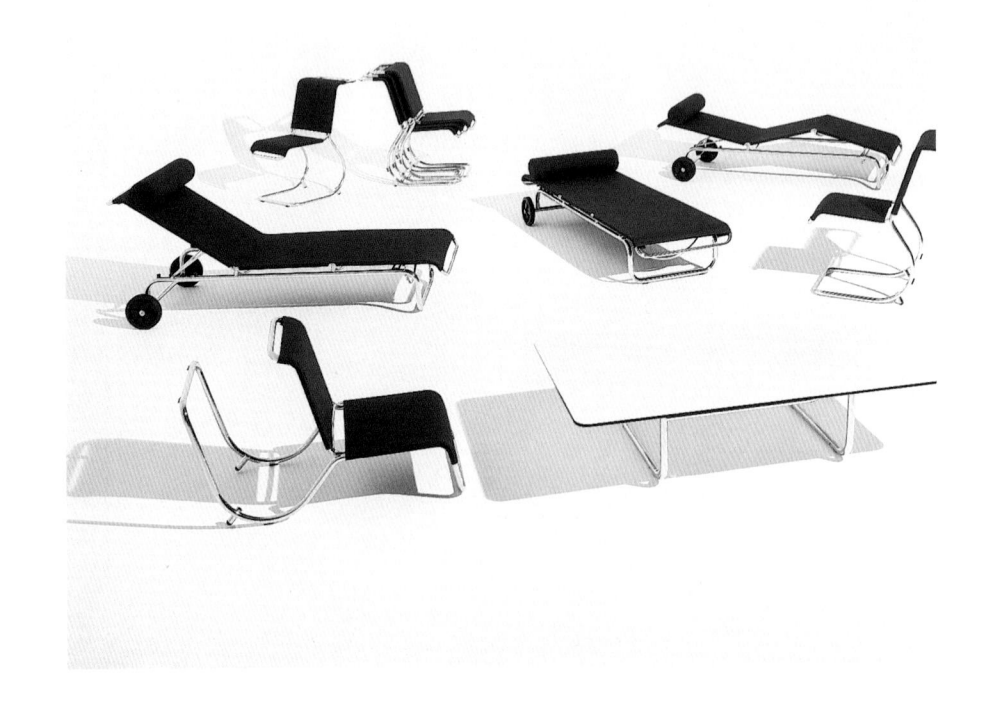

Furniture

Massimo Morozzi
Sofa – Cubista
polyurethane foam
h 72cm – w 180cm – d 108cm
h 28⅜in – w 70⅞in – d 42½in
Edra Mazzei – Italy

Simple geometries and bright colours are the basic ingredients of the Cubista range of seating. The joys of reconfiguration in one's home should of course be matched by the requisite amounts of space, and so for most this piece takes on the role of a signpost to an imagined way of life. This range of furniture harks back to the great Italian traditions of modern interiors wherein the centrepieces of what we think of as traditional domestic life – the armchair, sofa – are replaced by the building blocks of a relationship to furniture which few can afford or recognize from their own experience. – MH

Enrico Baleri
Elastic Seating – Lunella
polyurethane
h 25cm – di 58cm
h 9⁷/₈in – di 22⁷/₈in
Baleri Italia – Italy

Enrico Baleri's elastic seating is significant for two reasons. Not only does it build on the vernacular of Michael Young's experiments with elasticized polyurethane of a couple of years ago, but it also confirms the position of new, resilient fabrics in the palette of furniture designers. Of course the inherent properties of such fabrics means that the formal language of furniture is no longer tied to the characteristics and capabilities of the traditional frame. As with the pieces on the previous page, if furniture such as this can be moulded from durable materials, the formal languages of modern furniture should develop modern morphologies as a matter of course. The same thinking informed radical furniture design in Italy in the 1960s and 1970s: the difference now lies in the characteristics and quality of modern materials. – MH

Peter Karpf
Lounge Chair – OTO
laminated beech
h 75cm – w 80cm – d 60cm
h 29½in – w 31½in – d 23⅝in
Inredningsform/Iform – Sweden

Furniture

Mårten Claesson – Eero Koivisto – Ola Rune
Lounge Chair and Low Table – Bowie
birch or oak
chair – h 68cm – w 72cm – d 69cm
         h 26 ¾in – w 28 ⅜in – d 27 ⅞in
table – h 36cm – w 72cm – d 72cm
         h 14 ⅞in – w 28 ¾in – d 28 ¾in
David Design – Sweden

The forests of northern Europe, and in particular Scandinavia, provided the raw material for forms of furniture which are synonymous with modernity. The cross-lamination of birch and other veneers which are then moulded under heat and pressure creates a durable lightweight material which has built-in resilience. The material, although natural, is in this form a product of heavy machinery: from the veneer cutters in the sawmill to the hydraulic presses which give furniture like this its form. The combination of a lightweight, hardwearing natural material which is ideal for mass production with a still burgeoning tradition of formal experimentation has led to pieces such as these. There is a strong argument on this evidence for the identification of a European machine-based vernacular furniture. – MH

Antonio Citterio
Armchair – 637.98
thermoformed mesh – chromed aluminium
h 68cm – w 76cm – d 74cm
h 26¾in – w 29⅞in – d 29⅛in
B & B Italia – Italy

Furniture

Citterio's rather modernistic chrome and mesh chair recalls the studiedly modern aesthetic of the 1980s when even Eames' aluminium group chairs were available in a chrome and black, masculinized mesh. No doubt it is still possible to find some offices and homes in Europe where such an aesthetic holds sway, but as with any style the lure of such decorative simplicity is bound to diminish the more overused it becomes. This chair is interesting nevertheless for the thermoformed mesh seat, an element that connects the chair to the tradition of the plywood chairs on the previous pages. Perhaps over the next sixty years, the plasticity afforded by thermoformed mesh will lure designers in the same way that plywood has in the last. – MH

Paolo Rizzatto
Folding Chair – Clac
die-cast aluminium – tubular steel – thermoplastics
h 74cm – w 50cm – d 52cm
h 29¹/₈in – w 19⁵/₈in – d 20¹/₂in
Alias – Italy

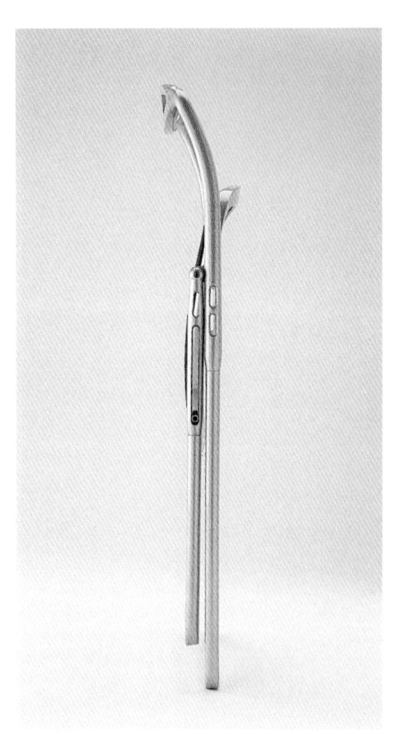

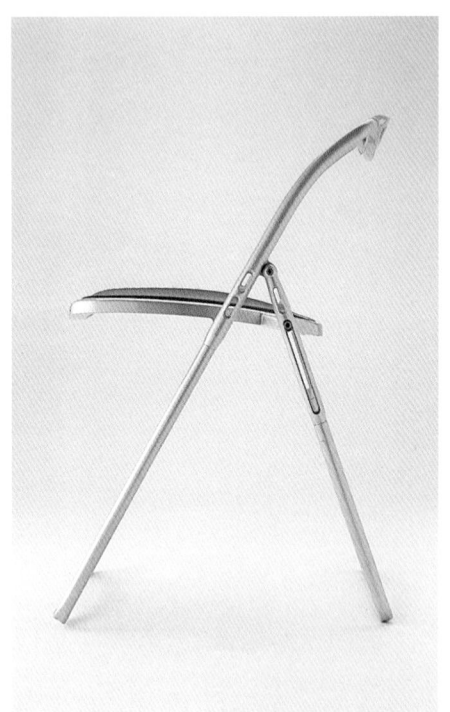

The two chairs shown on these pages contain thermo-moulded elements. The principal difference between the designs is in the materials used. The Clac chair uses die-cast aluminium, tubular steel and thermoplastics. The 290F uses beech thermo-moulded along what are now traditional lines by the Thonet organization. Although the form of Clac is modern, there is an economy of thought inherent in the 290F which is somehow more modern still. The use of one predominant material and the intelligent cutting of the seat from the back element during manufacture means that this chair demands less in the way of understanding from those who come across it. This is not to say that Clac is an inferior product. Clac's strengths clearly lie in its slim profile once folded away, and the materials used make it light and therefore portable; the handle also doubles as a backrest. – MH

Furniture

Wulf Schneider
Chair – 290F
moulded beechwood – bentwood – die-cast aluminium
h 80cm – w 55cm – d 51cm
h 31½in – w 21⅝in – d 20in
Gebrüder Thonet – Germany

Terence Woodgate
Chair/Pouffe/Table – Paulina
maple
chair – h 70cm – w 61cm – d 60cm
     h 27½in – w 24in – d 23⅝in
pouffe – h 37cm – w 61cm – d 52cm
     h 14⅝in – w 24in – d 20½in
table – h 37cm – w 61cm – d 52cm
     h 14⅝in – w 24in – d 20½in
Montina – Italy

Furniture

Michael Young
Chair – MY 68
beech or beech-stained wenge
h 80cm – w 38cm – d 38cm
h 31¹/₂in – w 15in – d 15in
Sawaya & Moroni – Italy

Jan Dranger for IKEA
Armchair – Rolig
recyclable plastic – cotton, nylon or polyester
h 72cm – w 70cm – d 70cm
h 28³/₈in – w 27½in – d 27½in
IKEA – Sweden

The idea of making a chair from recyclable materials is soon going to be a prerequisite for all large-scale manufacturers of office and domestic furniture. IKEA's place on the high street the world over demands perhaps a greater sensitivity to the issues and problems of environmental responsibility than might be expected from the makers of select and one-off designs in quirky materials. At best, a large company in IKEA's position can try to marry innovative design languages with environmental responsibility. But such responsibility goes far beyond the marketing of new furniture as 'recyclable'. Instead, environmental responsibility encompasses a complete responsibility for a product's impact on the world from the cradle to the grave. – MH

Furniture

Hella Jongerius
Stool
porcelain
h 50cm – w 50cm – d 20cm
h 19⅝in – w 19⅝in – d 7⅞in
Droog Design – The Netherlands

A porcelain stool is akin to a Dadaist joke, but as this product comes from the increasingly well-regarded Droog Design, that's more or less OK. It's not even as if porcelain is an unusual material on which to sit. We have been sitting on it in our WCs for more than a century. The displacement of familiar materials into unfamiliar territories and usages is in itself not new: think of Joe Colombo and Gaetano Pesce. Such subtlety in an execution like this, however, most certainly is. – MH

Piero Lissoni
Chair – Paper
fabric – wood
h 76cm – w 57.5cm – d 47cm
h 29 7/8in – w 22 5/8in – d 18 1/2in
Cappellini – Italy

Furniture

Uwe Fischer
Chair – Tama
plastic – aluminium – wenge/plywood or birch
h 80cm – w 56cm – d 52cm
h 31½in – w 22in – d 20½in
B & B Italia – Italy

Mario Bellini
Chair
polymer composite – glass fibre
h 84cm – w 44cm – d 46cm
h 33in – w 17³⁄₈in – d 18¹⁄₈in
Heller – USA

Furniture

Christian Steiner
Chair – Delta
wood – multiplex
h 81.5cm – w 44cm – d 56.5cm
h 32in – w 17 3/8in – d 22 1/4in
Schmidinger – Austria

Jorge Pensi
Stacking Chair – Hola
metal – polypropylene
h 82cm – w 57cm – d 54cm
h 32 1/4in – w 22 3/8in – d 21 1/2in
Kusch & Co. Sitzmöbelwerke – Germany

Furniture

Jorge Pensi
Chair – Temps
cherrywood or beechwood
h 78.5cm – w 41.5cm – d 49.5cm
h 30⅞in – w 16⅜in – d 19½in
Punt Mobles – Spain

Vico Magistretti
Armchair – Pollack
steel – polyurethane – aluminium
h 76cm – w 59cm – d 49cm
h 30in – w 23¼in – d 19¼in
Kartell – Italy

Carlo Bimbi and Paolo Romoli
Chair – Blitz
aluminium – polypropylene – leather
h 80cm – w 45cm – d 51cm
h 31½in – w 17¾in – d 20in
Segis – Italy

Furniture

Yrjö Kukkapuro
Chair – 552
tubular steel – birch plywood – upholstery
h 84.5cm – w 55cm – d 57cm
h 33¼in – w 21⅝in – d 22⅜in
Avarte – Finland

Stefano Giovannoni
Table – Bombo
steel – polypropylene
h 65cm/90cm – di 55cm
h 25½in/35⅜in – di 21⅝in
Magis – Italy

David Khouri
Stacking Cushions – TV Time
foam – vinyl – MDF – veneer
h 45.7cm – w 58.4cm – l 58.4cm
h 18in – w 23in – l 23in
Comma – USA
prototype

Traditionally, it has always been the designers working on space-saving and utility furniture who have determined the rules governing stacking furniture and the way it works. The rules which have grown out of this century's fascination with the ability to stack are about due for a revision. On these pages, pieces from Sweden and the USA point towards the potential of a new morphology for stacking furniture. In the case of the stacking cushions, the new form eschews the traditional tangle of legs and table tops for a more logical stacking of simple soft shapes around a central supportive element. IKEA's stools on the other hand clearly take their initiative from the way that packing crates stack within each other. – MH

Furniture

Knut and Marianne Hagberg
Stool – Patrull
injection-moulded polypropylene
h 13cm – w 33cm – l 19cm
h 5⅛in – w 13in – l 7½in
IKEA – Sweden

Karim Rashid
Chair with Removable Ottoman – Loungin
chrome – urethane foam
h 107cm – w 65cm – d 105cm
h 42½in – w 25¾in – d 41½in
Idee Co. – Japan

A footrest which can be reconfigured into a headrest seems at first glance like one of those innovations which will sit happily in the corner having been reconfigured only twice before the prospect of pulling out the footrest to make it a headrest once again begins to look like a little too much trouble – this chair may be an exception as the ease of reconfiguration speaks for itself. There is also, for the moment at least, a pleasingly contemporary geometry about the elements and the way they are brought together. – MH

Furniture

Jorge Pensi
Dining Chair – Duna
enamelled aluminium – plastic – polyurethane
h 84cm – w 57cm – d 57cm
h 33in – w 22³⁄₈in – d 22³⁄₈in
Cassina – Italy

Philippe Starck
Chair – La Marie
transparent polycarbonate
Kartell – Italy
prototype

The prolific nature of Starck's approach to his work means that there is rarely an edition of the *International Design Yearbook* which doesn't contain a piece of his work. What is exceptional this year is the choice of the material, although at the time of going to press it was unclear, no pun intended, whether or not this piece was to be a full production piece or a prototype designed to reveal the structure of the chair to those who see Starck's work as dealing principally with the cosmetic outer face of products. – MH

Thomas Sandell
Table – Miami
thermoformed Corian – aluminium – plastic
h 43cm – w 157cm – d 44cm
h 16 7/8in – w 61 7/8in – d 17 3/8in
B & B Italia – Italy

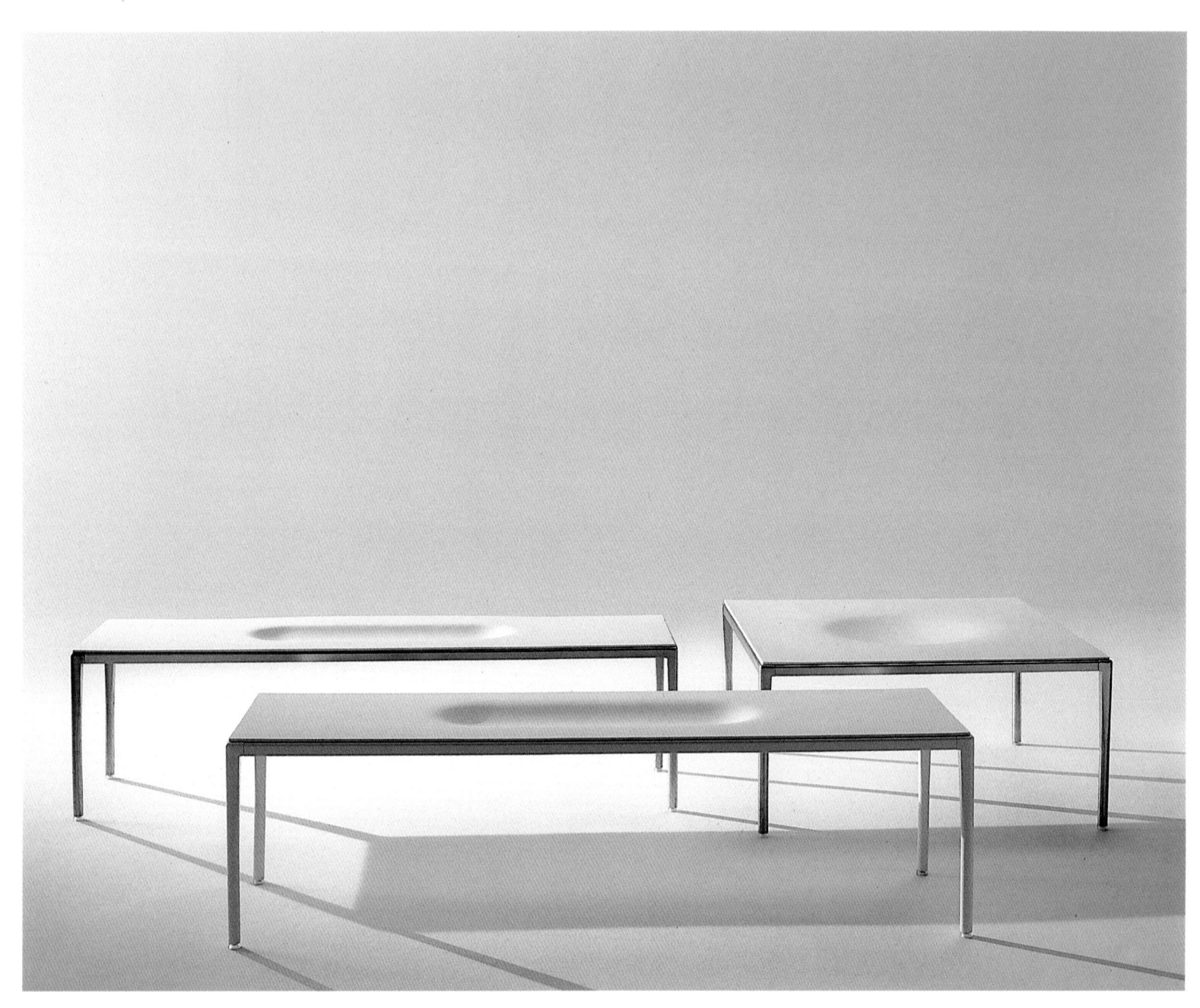

Furniture

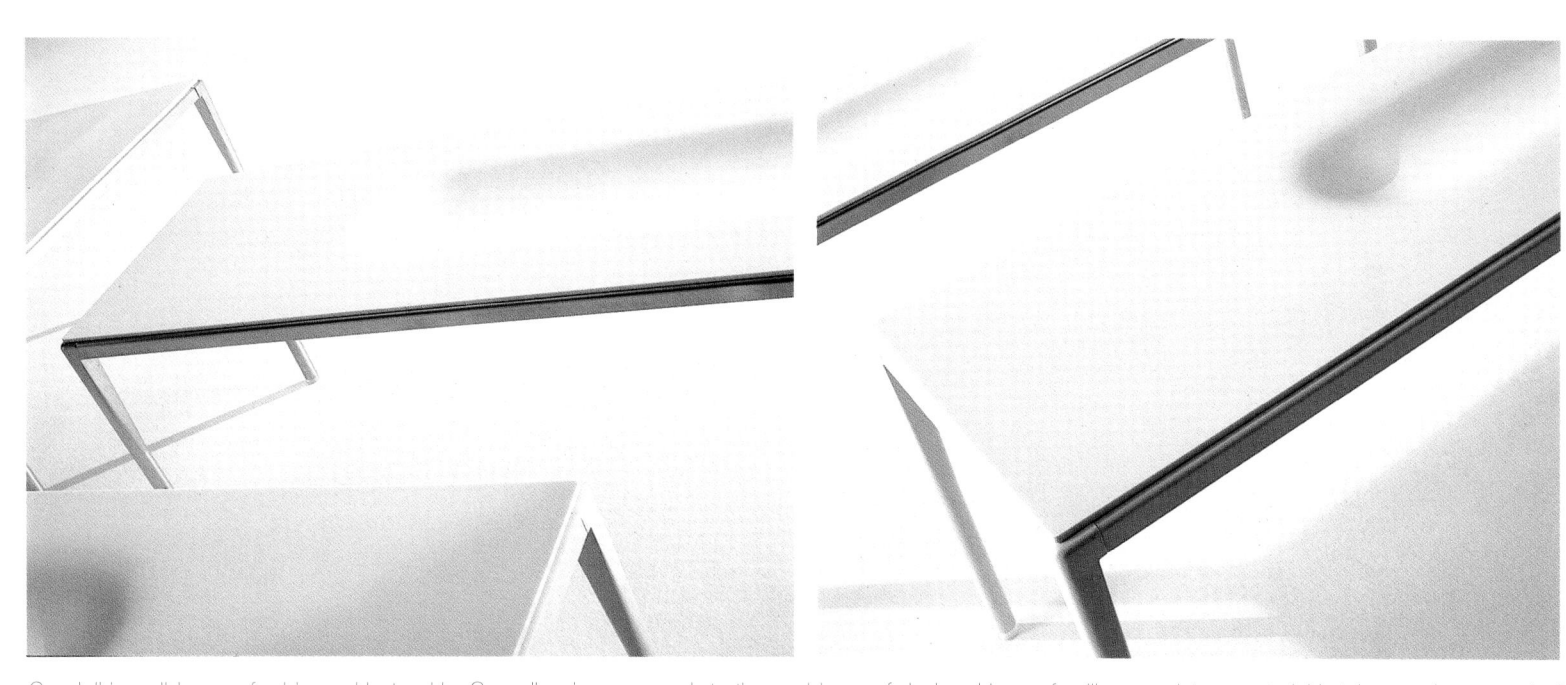

Sandell is well-known for his cool but quirky Scandinavian approach to the problems of design. Here a familiar proprietary material is taken and represented as an integral part of a finished design. The properties of Corian are well known to those with an interest in kitchen worktops: mouldable and reparable, cuttable and versatile with a density and mass which suggests a far more expensive material than it actually is, Corian inhabits a plastic netherworld somewhere between wood and real stone. In this manifestation Sandell has brought out the utility inherent in the material. Furthermore, the idea of a table with an integral fruitbowl – which could also hold keys, coins and the detritus of everyday life – would be an appealing one to anyone with the space and the inclination to buy a table which can be cleaned and maintained with ease. – MH

Ron Arad
Table – Konx
glass – silver – metal
h 34cm – w 120cm – d 80cm
h 13 3/8in – w 47 1/4in – d 31 1/2in
Fiam – Italy

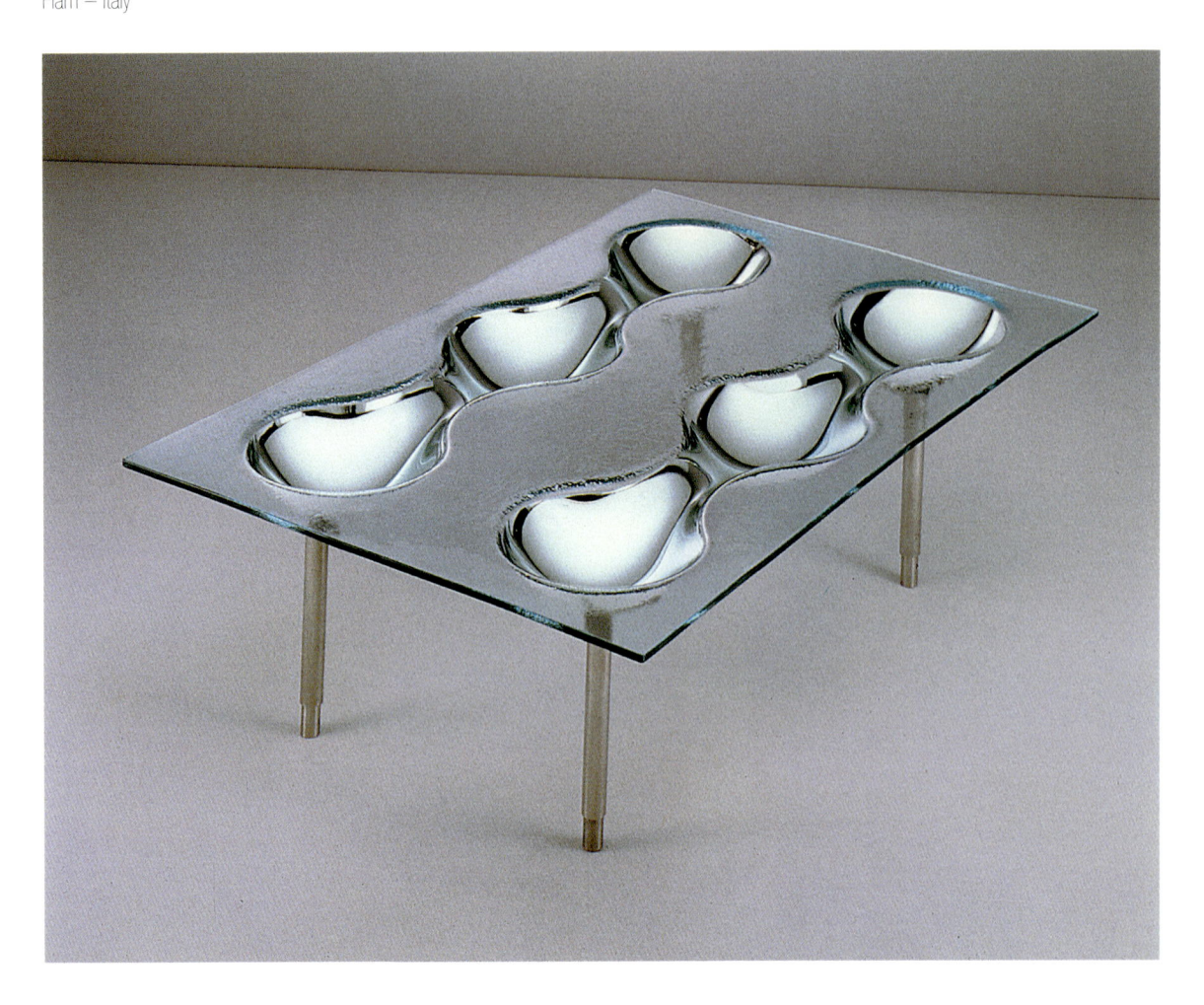

Furniture

Marc Newson
Table – Io
coated MDF – cable
h 71.8cm – d 131cm
h 28 1/4in – d 51 5/8in
B & B Italia – Italy

Angelo Mangiarotti
Table – T-Table
steel – glass
h 72.5cm – w 150cm – d 150cm
h 28½in – w 59in – d 59in
Baleri Italia – Italy

Furniture

Nanni/Bortolani
Set of Low Tables – Figura
aluminium – glass
h 53cm – w 70cm – d 70cm
h 20⅞in – w 27½in – d 27½in
Tonelli – Italy

Dillon Garris
Table – Pliade
anodized and perforated aluminium sheet
h 40cm – w 80cm – d 80cm
h 15¾in – w 31½in – d 31½in
Bourse VIA – France
prototype

The theme of transmutation appears throughout the selection this year. With this table the transparent panels slide around within the table frame creating different densities of colour. The degree to which this constitutes a reconfiguration is small compared to some other pieces within the book, but the principal point is that this kind of furniture allows itself to be interfered with. The very fact that it, like some other pieces, is designed to be remodelled at the owner's whim moves modern furniture into an area in which it is not enough to be decorative. The decorative possibilities of such pieces are subtly more diverse than those of pieces which rely entirely upon the qualities that are authored into the design by the designer. – MH

Shin and Tomoko Azumi
Stool=Shelf
maple – steel
h 43cm – w 35cm – d 32cm
h 16⅞in – w 13¾in – d 12⅝in
Azumi's – UK
limited batch production

Furniture

Achille Castiglioni
Coffee Table – Basellone
MDF – steel
h 45cm – w 135cm – d 85cm
h 17³⁄₄in – w 53¹⁄₈in – d 33¹⁄₂in
Zanotta – Italy

Barber Osgerby Associates
Table – Loop
bent beechwood or wenge
h 29cm – w 134cm – d 60cm
h 11³⁄₈in – w 52³⁄₄in – d 23⁵⁄₈in
Cappellini – Italy

BOA's Loop table is yet another statement of the 'curvilinear retro modern' style which seems to persist everywhere from Prague to London. Were the forms not quite so pleasing to the eye it would be tempting to identify a movement which was based entirely on the ability to draw a box with radial curves at either end. Instead, what we have here is a modern piece which smoothly captures a certain mood. Within this mood, the signifiers of modernity are less the traditional elements of pared down simplicity, than a mastery of rather complex geometries and as a corollary, manufacturing technologies. – MH

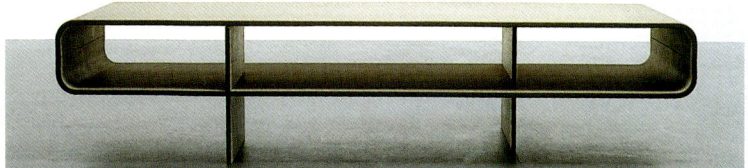

Vico Magistretti
Table – Trio
aluminium – MDF
h 70cm – di 70cm
h 27½in – di 27½in
De Padova – Italy

Ann Morsing and Beban Nord
Coffee Table – Cosmo
aluminium – oak
h 41cm – di 100cm
h 16⅛in – di 39⅜in
Box Design – Sweden

Furniture

Paul Daly
Table – Bullitt
plywood – laminate – beech
h 50cm – w 60cm – d 60cm
h 19⅝in – w 23⅝in – d 23⅝in
Paul Daly Design Studio – UK

Angelo Mangiarotti
Table – T-98
glass – wood
h 72cm – di 130cm
h 28⅜in – di 51⅛in
Novikos International – Italy

Stephen Burks
Room Divider – Screen
aluminium sheet – steel rod
h 160cm – d (module) 23cm
h 63in – d (module) 9in
Readymade – USA

Stephen Burks' metal room divider is a simple restatement of a functional tool for domestic living which gains a new life through an intelligent combination of colour and material. Coloured aluminium has a sheen about it which anyone who has ever bought cups or camping gear will recognize. – MH

Furniture

Konstantin Grcic
Clothes Stand – Hut Ab
ash – aluminium
h 184cm/200cm – w 63cm – d 12cm/63cm
h 72³/₈in/78³/₄in – w 24⁷/₈in – d 4⁷/₈in/24⁷/₈in
Nils Holger Moorman – Germany

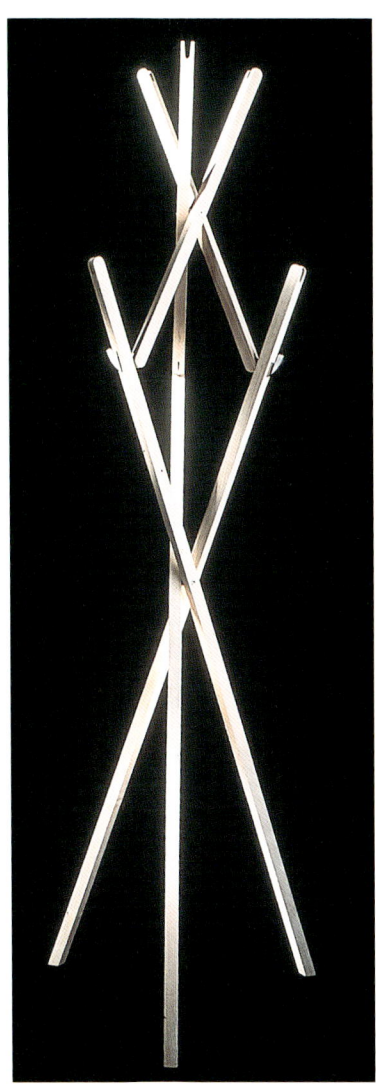

Christof Burtscher and Patrizia Bertolini
Shelves – Slim
birch
h 92–212cm – w 144cm – d 34cm
h 36¼–83½in – w 56⅝in – d 13⅜in
Atelier – Italy

Fabio Bortolani and Emilio Nanni
Shelves – Corner
birch
h 93cm – w 60cm – d 60cm
h 36⅝in – w 23⅝in – d 23⅝in
Atelier – Italy

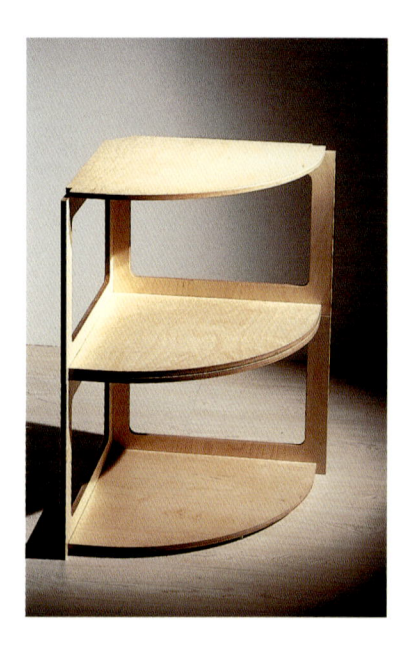

Furniture

Michael Sodeau
Wall Shelves – Duo
rosewood-veneered MDF
h 100cm – w 100cm – d 30cm
h 39⅜in – w 39⅜in – d 11¾in
Michael Sodeau Partnership – UK
limited batch production

Effective use of simple orthogonal geometries is always a refreshing sight. It is also interesting to see the development of Michael Sodeau's visual and formal language post Inflate. The simple appearance of this piece belies the complexity of its manufacture where rosewood is veneered on to MDF. The use of rosewood adds a textural richness to the plainly rigorous, and yet intriguingly composed form. – MH

Olgoj Chorchoj
Shelves – Matrioschka
plywood – duralumin – stainless steel
h 150cm – w 50cm – d 37cm
h 59in – w 19⅝in – d 14⅝in
Konsepti – Czech Republic
limited batch production

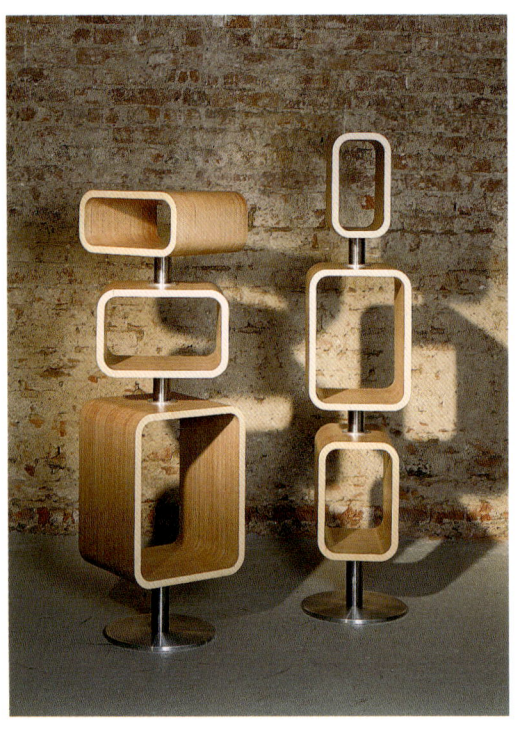

Lloyd Schwan
Hanging Wall System – Minus
wood – lacquer
box – h 36cm – w 50cm – d 28cm
  h 14⅛in – w 19⅝in – d 11in
cd holder – h 18cm – w 80cm – d 18cm
  h 7in – w 31½in – d 7in
bookshelf – h 26cm – w 100cm – d 27cm
  h 10½in – w 39⅜in – d 10⅝in
Box Design – Sweden

The complex geometry and manufacturing techniques – lamination and cutting – which go to make these pieces from the diverse economies and design worlds of the Czech Republic and Sweden somehow take a backseat when we witness the seemingly ubiquitous modern curve once again. So smooth and simplistically beguiling are these forms that the layman would be hard pressed to decide why these pieces were worthy of note. In the case of the Czechs, it's worth expanding a little on why a comment is worthwhile. These pieces represent yet another stage in the rehabilitation of that nation and its inventive designers into the fabric of modern European life. The appearance of Czech design in these pages is a sign that, finally, in terms of small scale and short run production of goods for the home, the Czechs can hold their own with any European competitor. They perhaps have the added advantage that for the moment at least, their work is exotic enough to be sought after solely for the reason that it comes from a place which has not been widely associated with modern design in recent times. This situation is bound to change sooner rather than later and it will be interesting to keep an eye on the way things develop in future years. – MH

Furniture

Carl Pickering and Claudio Lazzarini
Modular System consisting of three elements – Isotrop
cherrywood – ebonized cherrywood
X – h 105cm – w 210cm – d 35cm
　　h 41 3/8 in – w 82 5/8 in – d 13 3/4 in
Y – h 35cm – w 210cm – d 70cm
　　h 13 3/4 in – w 82 5/8 in – d 27 1/2 in
Z – h 70cm – w 210cm – d 35cm
　　h 27 1/2 in – w 82 5/8 in – d 13 3/4 in
Acierno – Italy

Carl Pickering and Claudio Lazzarini come from an architectural perspective to create a system of storage for the home which is serious as well as being simple. The collision of planes, masses and voids which comes about in the installation of a piece of furniture such as this recalls the rigour and inventiveness of minimalist composition. With a modular system, the task of configuration and hence decoration is left to the consumer. The idea that something as minimally impactful as a series of orthogonal boxes can be decorative is not new; this method of deployment, however, is. – MH

Benny Mosimann/Wogg
Sideboard – Wogg 18
polycarbonate – melamine
h 44cm/79cm/114cm – w 148cm – d 37cm
h 17³⁄₈in/31¹⁄₈in/44⁷⁄₈in – w 58¹⁄₄in – d 14⁵⁄₈in
Wogg – Switzerland

Alfredo Häberli and Christophe Marchand
Shelving System – Sec
die-cast and extruded aluminium – sheet steel – glass – Carrara marble – acrylic
module – h 16cm/25cm/36cm – w 50cm/100cm – d 30cm/45cm
h 6¹⁄₄in/9⁷⁄₈in/14¹⁄₈in – w 19⁵⁄₈in/39³⁄₈in – d 11³⁄₄in/17³⁄₄in
Alias – Italy

Furniture

Bruno Fattorini
Shelving System – Minima 40
anodized aluminium
module – h 38cm – w 34.5cm/70cm – d 40cm
h 15in – w 13⅝in/27½in – d 15¾in
MDF Italia – Italy

Alberto Meda and Paolo Rizzatto
Shelves – Partner
plastic – aluminium
h 137cm – w 103cm – d 35cm
h 53⅞in – w 40⅝in – d 13¾in
Kartell – Italy

Wogg
Shelving System – Wogg 22
high-density fibreboard – high-pressure laminate – aluminium
h 214.2cm – w 30cm/60cm – d 33cm
h 84 1/3in – w 11 3/4in/23 5/8in – d 13in
Wogg – Switzerland

Furniture

Roberto Feo
Shelving System – Plug It
MDF
back unit – h 60cm – w 60cm – d 9cm
    h 23⅝in – w 23⅝in – d 3⅝in
box – h 27cm – w 52cm – d 20cm
    h 10⅝in – w 20½in – d 7⅞in
prototype

Fernando and Humberto Campana
Modular Stand – Labyrinth
aluminium
h 140cm – w 140cm – d 40cm
h 55⅛in – w 55⅛in – d 15¾in
Campana Objetos – Brazil
limited batch production

Plug It represents yet another facet of the phenomenon of the simple object presenting a range of different compositional possibilities with which to achieve its decorative potential. In this case Roberto Feo's shelves combine the decorative/functional background with a functional/decorative foreground. The resulting composition is as much the owner's responsibility as it is the designer's. – MH

Lighting

At its most extravagant, design for lighting in the home pre-supposes the use of the home as something akin to a stage set. At the other end of the spectrum, domestic lighting delivers the most functional and, if well executed, unobtrusive addition to the home. The delivery of electricity into the domestic environment has effected the greatest changes in the way we live. Our times of waking and sleeping, what we do for entertainment, our very modes of living have been shaped by our relationship to the current available to us through the wall or ceiling. But the manufacture of electricity for our use is one of the primary contributors to the environmental difficulties with which we are now beset. It is interesting then to note that there is at least a sign that designers are addressing the idea of lighting which does not draw continually on generated electricity, but which harnesses the power of the sun. This is an important break with convention. Domestic lighting which does not draw upon the national grid – in whichever nation – is a project which designers, manufacturers and engineers should look at with the same application as they have the energy-saving bulb. To do so will ensure that the most decorative arm of hi-tech manufacture will eventually transcend its largely cosmetic role.

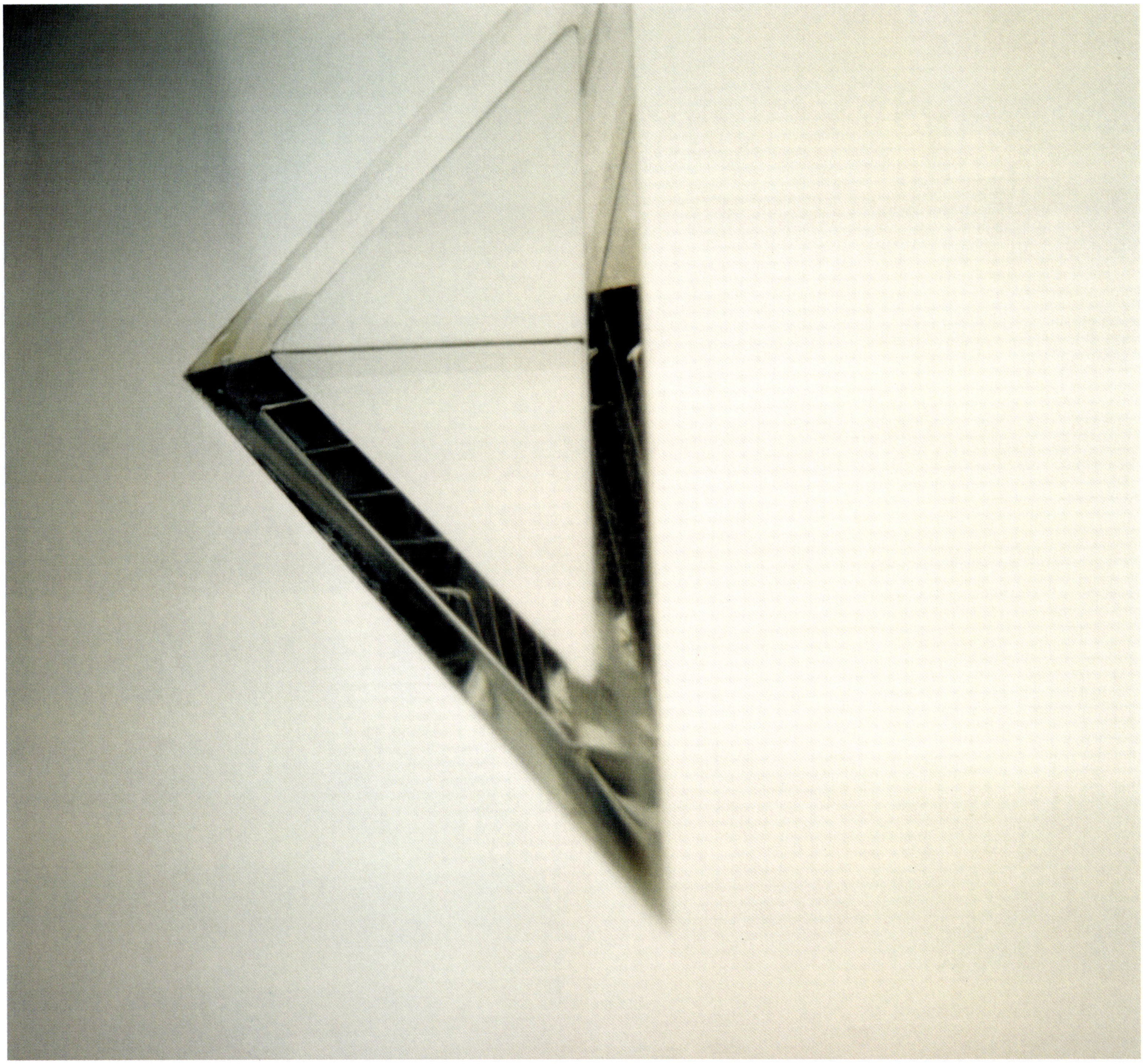

Achille Castiglioni
Suspension Light – Diabolo
aluminium
1 x 150w bulb
h min. 94cm – di 40cm
h min. 37in – di 15¾in
Flos – Italy

Lighting

Ross Lovegrove
Lighting Series– Pod Lens
injection-moulded polycarbonate
40w E14/23w E27 bulb
h 28.5cm/200cm – di 10.5cm
h 11⅛in/78¾in – di 4⅛in
Luceplan – Italy

Ross Lovegrove
Lighting Series– Solar Bud
3 red LEDs
h 37cm – di 15cm
h 14⅝in – di 5⅞in
Luceplan – Italy

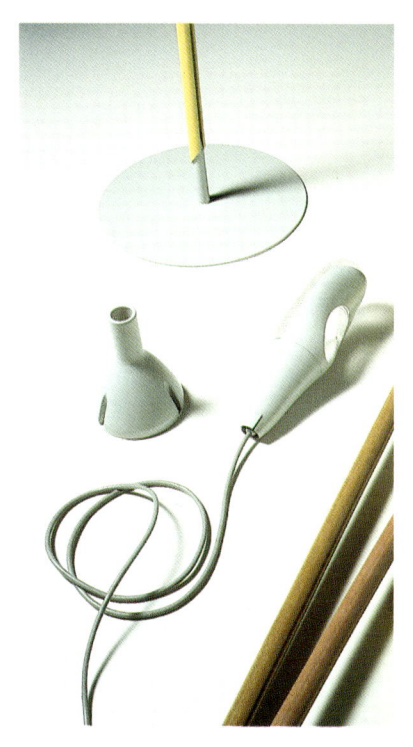

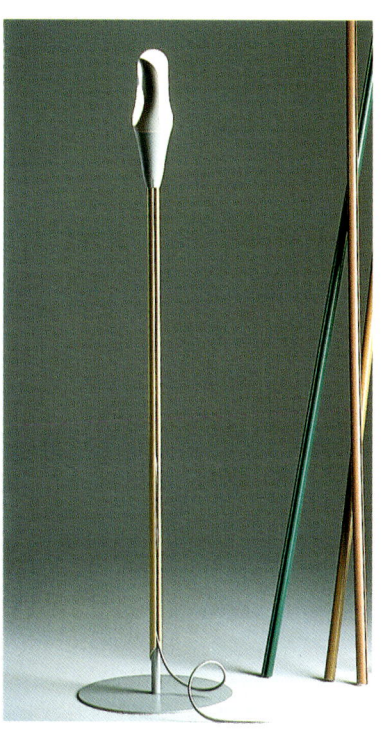

Innovation on this scale is rare in any form of design, but Ross Lovegrove's lighting system takes the idea of light and light energy quite a long way away from the simple lightbulb, its link with the power station and its domestic role. Designed to create a chain of lights which are powered by solar energy, the Solar Bud collects its power from a solar panel which recharges the battery. The whole light can be jammed into the earth to define pathways or other garden features. The obvious green appeal of this product should ensure a healthy degree of interest and a possible new direction for the generation of families of domestic lighting which depend upon the sun for their energy supply rather than a two-pin hole in the wall. Elemental and self contained, the Solar Bud is a timely re-interpretation of a technology which, in terms of widespread domestic usage, has been rather left on the sidelines. The 'Do It Yourself' Pod Lens is also suitable for outdoor use, featuring a kit of parts which allow the light to be stuck in the ground or arranged as fence posts or hung in clusters from the trees. – MH

Marta Laudani and Marco Romanelli
Suspension Light – Floor Lamp – Table Lamp
sand-blasted Murano glass – glazed anodized metal
suspension light – di 24cm di 9⅜in
　　　　　　　　1 x 150w bulb
floor lamp – h 180cm – di 24cm
　　　　　　h 70⅞in – di 9⅜in
　　　　　　1 x 250w bulb
table lamp – h 35cm – di 24cm
　　　　　　h 13¾in – di 9⅜in
　　　　　　1 x 250w bulb
Oluce – Italy

Sebastian Bergne
Suspension Light – Lid
sand-blasted glass – aluminium
4 x max. 60w bulbs/4 x max. 75w bulbs
di 40cm/50cm
di 15¾in/19⅝in
Oluce – Italy

Lighting

Roberto Pamio
Suspension Light – Ivette
metal – glass
100w incandescent bulb
h max. 230cm – di 38cm
h max. 90 1/2in – di 15in
Fabbian Illuminazione – Italy

On Design (Andreas Ostwald – Klaus Nolting)
Suspension Light – Aphaia
opaline glass – lacquered metal
150w halogen bulb
h 100cm/170cm – w 62cm – d 30cm
h 39 3/8in/66 7/8in – w 24 3/8in – d 11 7/8in
ClassiCon – Germany

Michele de Lucchi
Suspension Light – Aleppo 44
thermoplastic resin – aluminium – glass
max. 150w incandescent bulb
h 65–225cm – di 44cm
h 25 5/8–88 5/8in – di 17 3/8in
Artemide – Italy

Winfried Scheuer
Edison Light
aluminium
max. 60w bulb
h 12cm – di 14cm
h 4¾in – di 5½in
Aero Wholesale – UK

Michele de Lucchi
Table Lamp – Tokio
metal – Murano glass
max. 60w spot R63 bulb
h 32cm – di 16cm
h 12⅝in – di 6¼in
Produzione Privata – Italy

Lighting

Ilkka Suppanen
Suspension Light – Roll Light
aluminium – mylar film – carbon fibre
70w halogen bulb
h 80cm – w 140cm – l variable
h 31½in – w 55⅛in – l variable
prototype

Philip Baldwin and Monica Guggisberg
Hanging Floor Light – Abacus
hand-blown glass
5 x max. 40w bulbs
h 189–589cm – di 19cm
h 74⅜–231⅞in – di 7½in
Venini – Italy

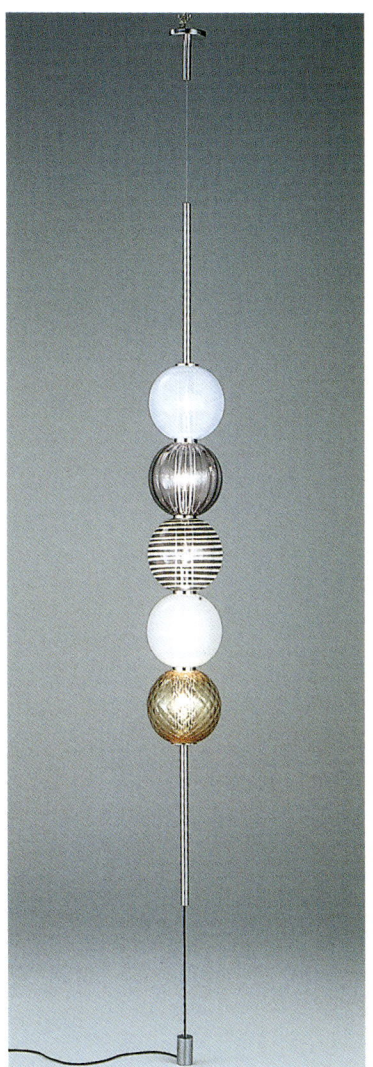

Miguel Vieira Baptista
Light from the Terra Collection – T8
ceramic
max. 40w bulb
h 12cm
h 4¾in
Authentics – Germany

Sebastian Bergne
Light from the Terra Collection – T13
ceramic
max. 40w bulb
h 22cm – di 11cm
h 8⅝in – di 4⅜in
Authentics – Germany

The avowed aim of Authentics is to reveal the properties and the beauties of particular materials: the idea is to make material decorative without decorating it. The concentration is therefore on the form and the function – an old but effective rubric – and not on the development of applied decorative techniques. Strange then, that these pieces should evoke a pair of binoculars, some underpants and a birdhouse. – MH

Lighting

Fernando Brízio
Light from the Terra Collection – T4
ceramic
max. 40w bulb
h 12cm
h 4 3/4 in
Authentics – Germany

Pedro Silva Dias
Light from the Terra Collection – T11
ceramic
max. 40w bulb
h 15cm – di 15cm
h 5 7/8 in – di 5 7/8 in
Proto Design – Portugal

Neil Poulton
Suspension Light and Wall Light – Surf System
extruded aluminium – polycarbonate
T5 linear fluorescent bulb
h 3.2cm – w 18cm – l 120cm/150cm
h 1¼in – w 7in – l 47¼in/59in
Artemide – Italy

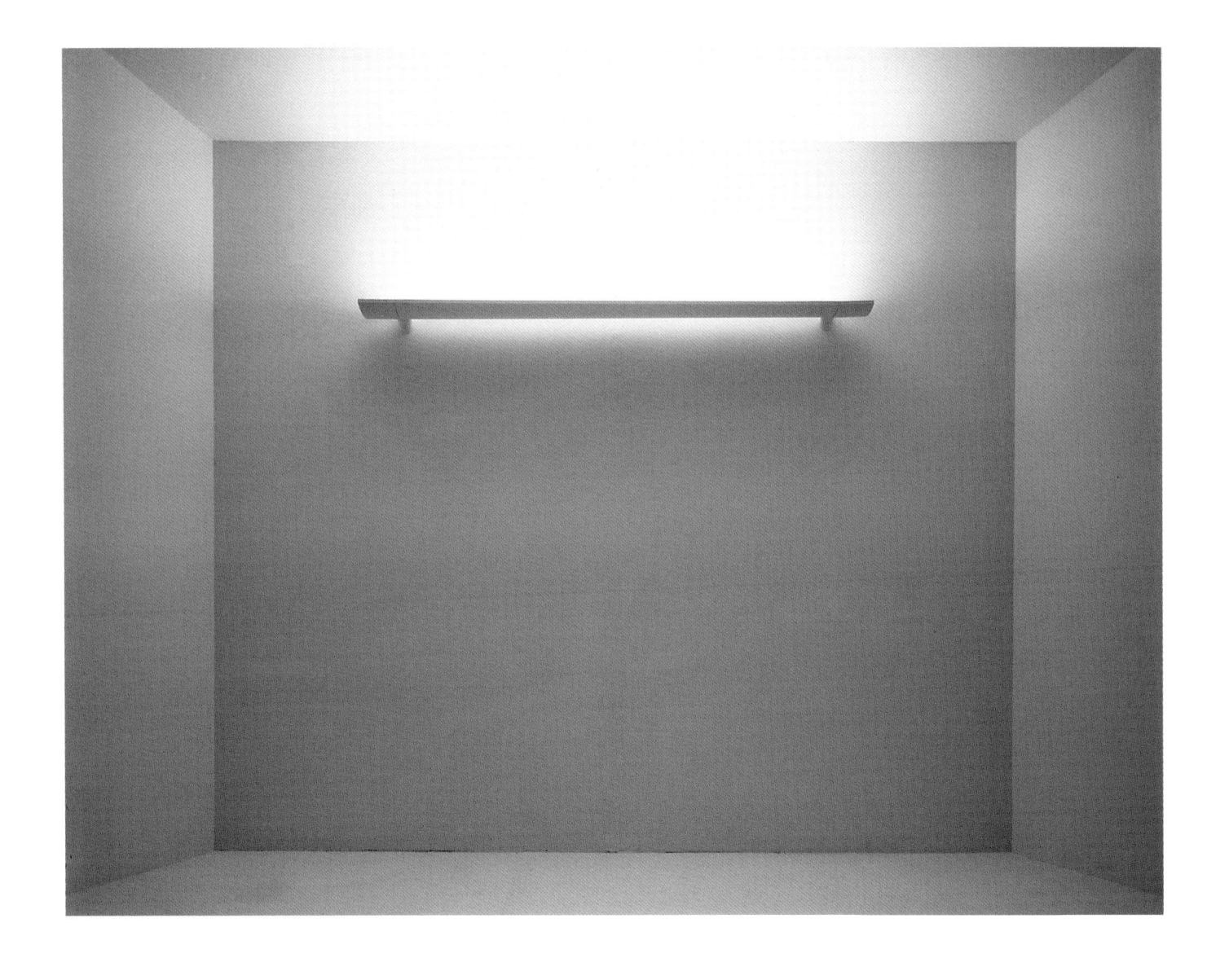

Lighting

Philippe Starck
Desk Light – Archimoon Classic
metal
1 x 60w bulb
h 30.4–56.6cm – w 57–96.6cm
h 12–22 1/4in – w 22 3/8–38in
Flos – Italy

Lighting

In addressing the Anglepoise-style lamp as a project Philippe Starck has lent his considerable reputation to a task which is difficult to fathom. Anglepoise type lamps have long been acknowledged as particularly finely wrought designs. Sound engineering allegedly inspired by the workings of the human arm has been used as the basis for desk lamps since the 1920s. Improvements in materials and bulb technologies aside, the principles behind such lamps remain unchanged. This then is another well-designed version of the original. — MH

Alberto Meda and Paolo Rizzatto
Lighting Series – Fortebraccio
steel – zamak – thermoplastics – aluminium
100w incandescent bulb, 60w halogen bulb or 18w energy-saving bulb
l (of arms) 35cm/45cm
l (of arms) 9⅜in/17¾in
Luceplan – Italy

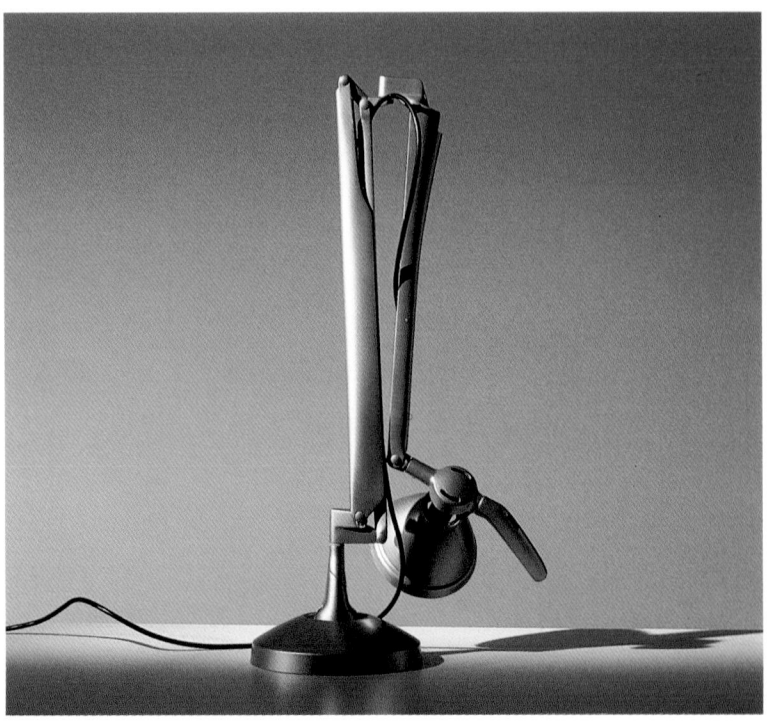

Likewise, this version of the Anglepoise uses a tried and tested configuration with the key difference that many of the working parts are concealed within a fairing. This small but important detail – adding the skin to the skeleton as it were – has moved the form of the lamp firmly into the end of the twentieth century after decades of stasis. – MH

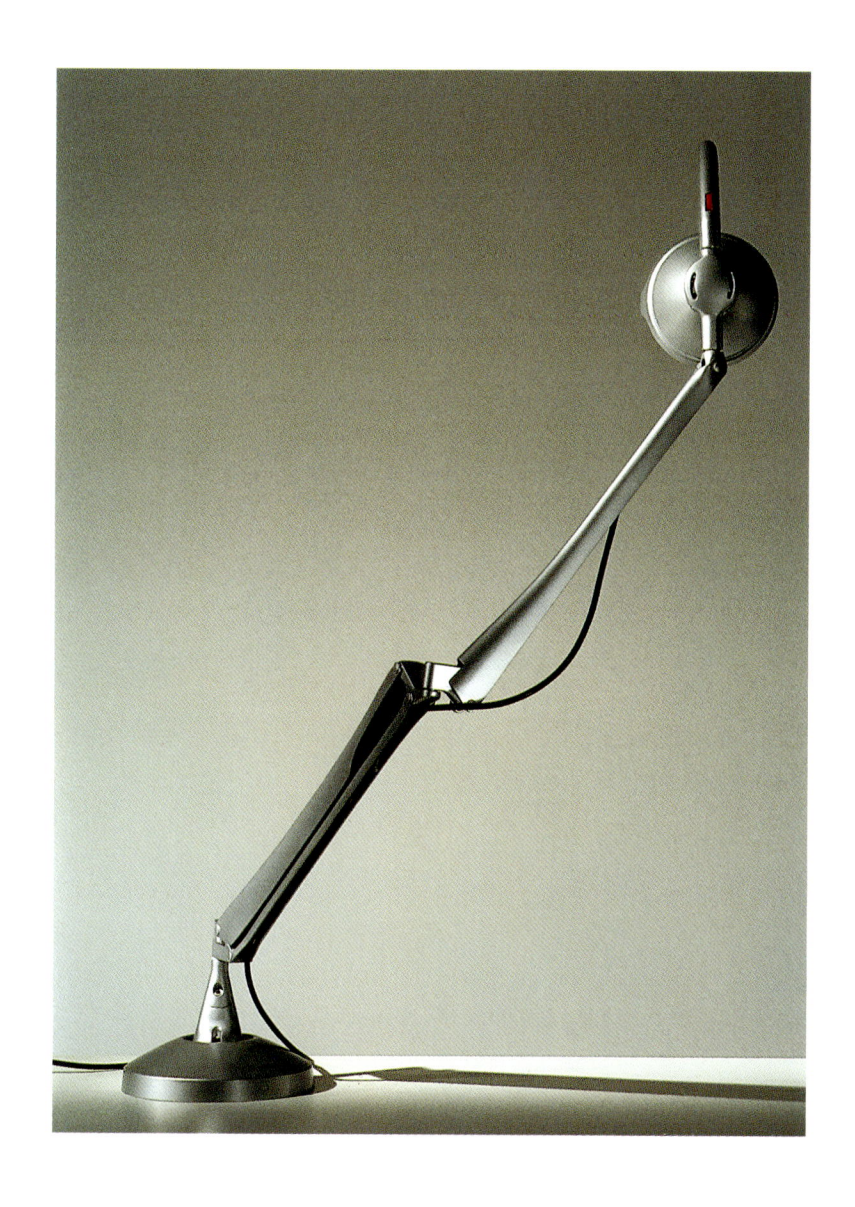

Lighting

Perry A. King and Santiago Miranda
Desk Task Light for use with VDUs – Miss Moneypennie
moulded plastic – aluminium – steel
13w compact fluorescent bulb
h 24–54cm – d (reach) 40–80cm
h 9⅜–21¼in – d (reach) 15¾–31½in
Colebrook Bosson Saunders Products – UK

Lighting

Ann Morsing and Beban Nord
Lamp from the PJ Series
aluminium – steel
60w bulb
h 60cm/125cm
h 23⅝in/49¼in
Box Design – Sweden

Maarten Van Severen
Floor Lamp – U-line
aluminium
11w fluorescent tube
h 122cm – w 60cm
h 48in – w 23⅝in
Target Lighting – Belgium

Lighting

Christian Deuber (N2)
Floor Lamp – Havana
steel tube – aluminium – polycarbonate film
150w bulb
h 180cm – di 60cm
h 70⅞in – di 23⅝in
Pallucco Italia – Italy
prototype

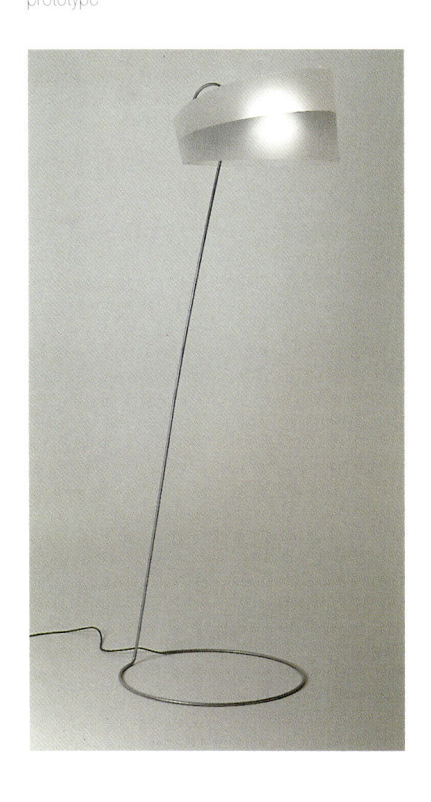

Ernesto Gismondi
Table Lamp – Miconos
polished chromium metal – blown glass
1 x 100w bulb
h 60cm – di 25cm
h 23⅝in – di 9⅞in
Artemide – Italy

Andrea Branzi
Floor Lamp – Quirino
lacquered metal – fabric
1 x 150w halogen bulb and 1 x 150w
incandescent globe or
1 x 150w halogen (E27) bulb
h 181cm – di 34cm
h 71¼in – di 13⅜in
Artemide – Italy

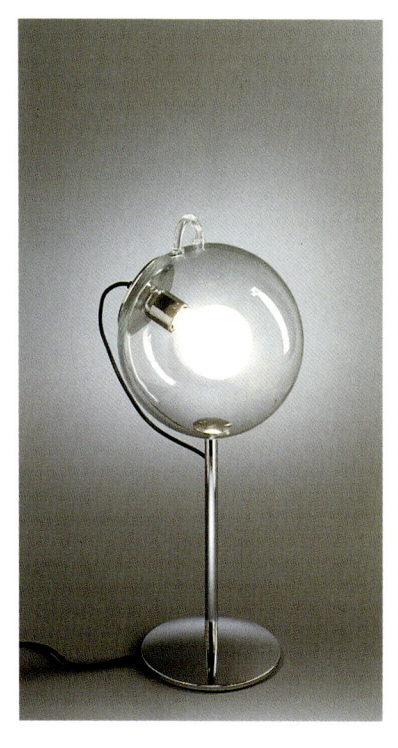

Herbert H. Schultes
Floor Lamp – Pilos
satin chrome-plated steel
250w halogen bulb
h 197cm – w 27cm
h 77½in – w 10⅝in
ClassiCon – Germany

Herbert H. Schultes
Floor Lamp – Numa
satin chrome-plated steel – opaline glass
100w bulb
h 114cm/154cm/194cm – w 27cm
h 44⅞in/60⅝in/76⅜in – w 10⅝in
ClassiCon – Germany

Lighting

Marcel Wanders
Floor Lamp from the Shadows Series
laminated textile
h 120cm/200cm – di 53cm/91cm
h 47¼in/78¾in – di 20⅞in/35⅞in
Cappellini – Italy

Marcel Wanders has been developing an approach to furniture and objects which depends heavily on the pun. The displacement of objects out of either their normal function or their normal size is a classic element of humour. Jokes are not universal, however, and so Wanders' problem is to find enough people who will appreciate the joke day in and day out when they are living with these studiedly quirky objects. – MH

Renaud Thiry
Table Lamp – Jour de Fête
nickel-coated brushed metal – PVC
60w incandescent bulb
h 27cm/35cm – di 25cm/35cm
h 10⅝in/13¾in – di 9⅞in/13¾in
Ligne Roset – France

Hans Peter Weidemann
Table Lamp – Luxy
Murano glass – metal
1 x 150w bulb and 2 x 40w bulbs
h 29cm/47cm – w 19cm/30cm
h 11⅜in/18½in – w 7½in/11⅞in
Oluce – Italy

Lighting

Hiroyuki Yamakado
Table Lamp – Champignon de Paris
glass
110/220w bulb
h 17cm – di 15cm/20cm
h 6⅝in – di 5⅞in/7⅞in
Yamakado – France

Giovanni D'Ambrosio
Table Lamp – Atmosfera
blown Murano glass
100w halogen bulb or 23w fluorescent bulb
h 41cm – w 36.5cm/30cm
h 16⅛in – w 14⅜in/11⅞in
Murano Due – Italy

Konstantin Grcic
Light from the Terra Collection – T7
ceramic
max. 60w bulb
h 20cm – di 15cm
h 7 7/8in – di 5 7/8in
Proto Design – Portugal

José Viana
Light from the Terra Collection – T5
ceramic
max. 40w bulb
h 20cm – di 6cm
h 7 7/8in – di 2 3/8in
Proto Design – Portugal

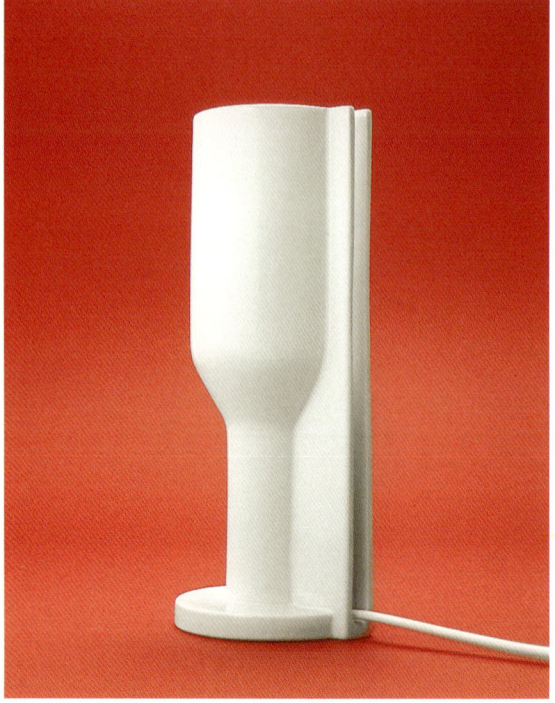

Lighting

Klaus Hackl
Multi-purpose Light – Pelle
aluminium – rubber
h 7cm – w 6cm – l 19cm
h 2¾in – w 2⅜in – l 7½in
limited batch production

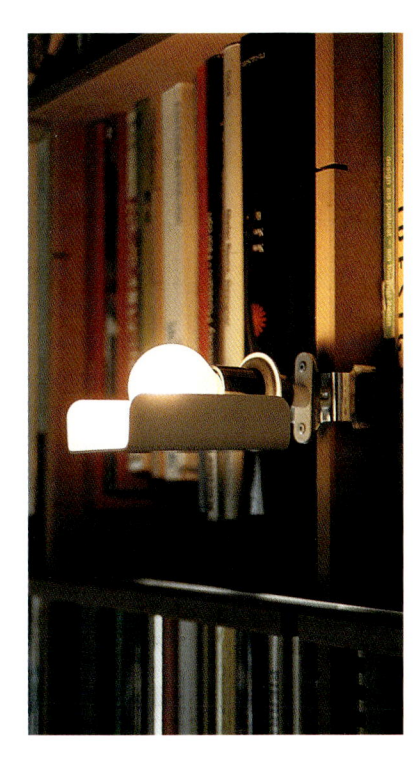

Antoine Cahen
Torch – SL Light
rubber-like plastic
4.5v standard battery
h 9cm – w 6.3cm – d 2cm
h 3½in – w 2½in – d ¾in
Les Ateliers du Nord – Switzerland

Lighting

Matsushita Electric Industrial Co. Ltd
Light Bulb – EFT15E28
electronic components – glass
15w bulb
h 13.7cm – di 6.0cm
h 5 3/8in – di 2 7/8in
Matsushita Electronic Industrial Co. – Japan

Fons Labohm and Patrick van de Voorde
Light Bulb – Philips Ecotone Ambiance
electronic components – glass
available as 5, 9 or 11w bulb
h 13.2cm – di 6.5cm
h 5 1/4in – di 2 5/8in
Philips Lighting – The Netherlands

Tableware

It would be tempting to think design for tableware offered the best opportunity for designers to execute the definitive design. After all, the conjunction between a human hand, a mouth and a fork – if not violently intended – should be determinable to the extent that the perfect fork should already exist. Equally, the number of good variations on a round white plate with a lip must be close to exhaustion. Accordingly, we must be only a short way away from the perfect dinner plate coming into existence. Drinking glasses have particular functions, it is true, but those for the water and the wine must have reached the point where they are near perfect. Strange then, that this most functional of categories should spawn, by and large, the most fanciful and clearly decorative designs. Perhaps because designing vessels has traditionally been allied to the crafts, the notion of glasses, plates and vessels of all kinds maintaining a kind of eternal plasticity seems, for the moment, acceptable.

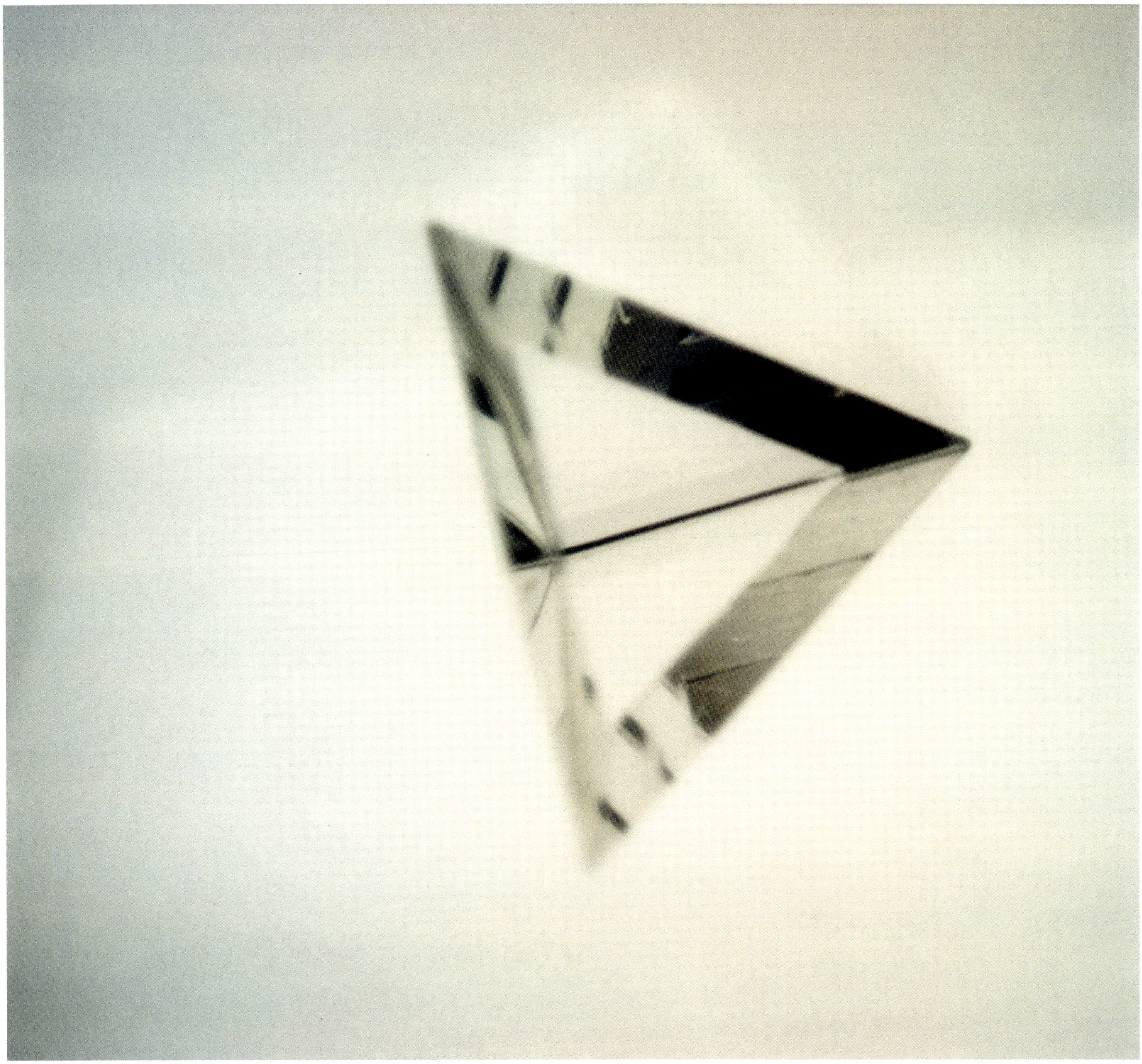

Isabel Hamm
Glass Bowl
lead crystal glass
h 5cm – di 36cm
h 2in – di 14 1/8in
Arcade – Italy
limited batch production

Tableware

Limited production batches of lead crystal glassware do not exactly sit easily with today's dominant ideology and idea of modern mass production. The archaic practices of small-scale luxury production are tempered here by a judicious attention to form and an eye for contemporary colour. When traditions such as the manufacture of vessels in lead crystal move forward in this way and embrace contemporary concerns, those traditions begin the process of ensuring their survival. — MH

Arnout Visser
Condensation Bowls
glass – water
h 8cm/12cm/18cm – di 12cm/18cm/24cm
h 3 1/8in/4 3/4in/7in – di 4 3/4in/7in/9 3/8in
Droog Design – The Netherlands
prototype

Arnout Visser
Drinking Glass – Optic Glass
glass
h 11cm – di 5cm
h 4 3/8in – di 2in
Droog Design – The Netherlands
prototype

Tableware

Martin Szekely
Perrier Glass
glass
h 13cm – di 8.5cm
h 5 1/8in – di 3 3/8in
Perrier (Nestlé) – France

Udo Posch
Vinegar/Oil Bottle – Downright
glass – cork
h 17cm – di 5cm/6.5cm
h 6 5/8in – di 2in/2 1/2in
Posch Collection – Germany

Rolf Sachs
Open-ended Vase
glass – rubber
h 39cm – di 11.5cm
h 15 3/8in – di 4 1/2in
A1 Laboratory Supplies – UK
limited batch production

Roberto and Ludovica Palomba
Vase – All
glass
h 70cm – di 23cm
h 27½in – di 9in
AllGlass – Italy

There is something about the processes of shaping glass when it is not blown or handworked that at best ensures an attention to simplicity of form. The material lends itself to objects which take their structural and formal integrity from the enforced clarity of their composition. In short, if pieces in glass are wrongly conceived and executed the unforgiving nature of the material reveals the flaws in the manufacture and ultimately in the ideas which led to the manufacture. – MH

Tableware

Marzia Chierichetti
Vase – Cubo
glass
h 52cm – w 11cm
h 20½in – w 4⅜in
AllGlass – Italy

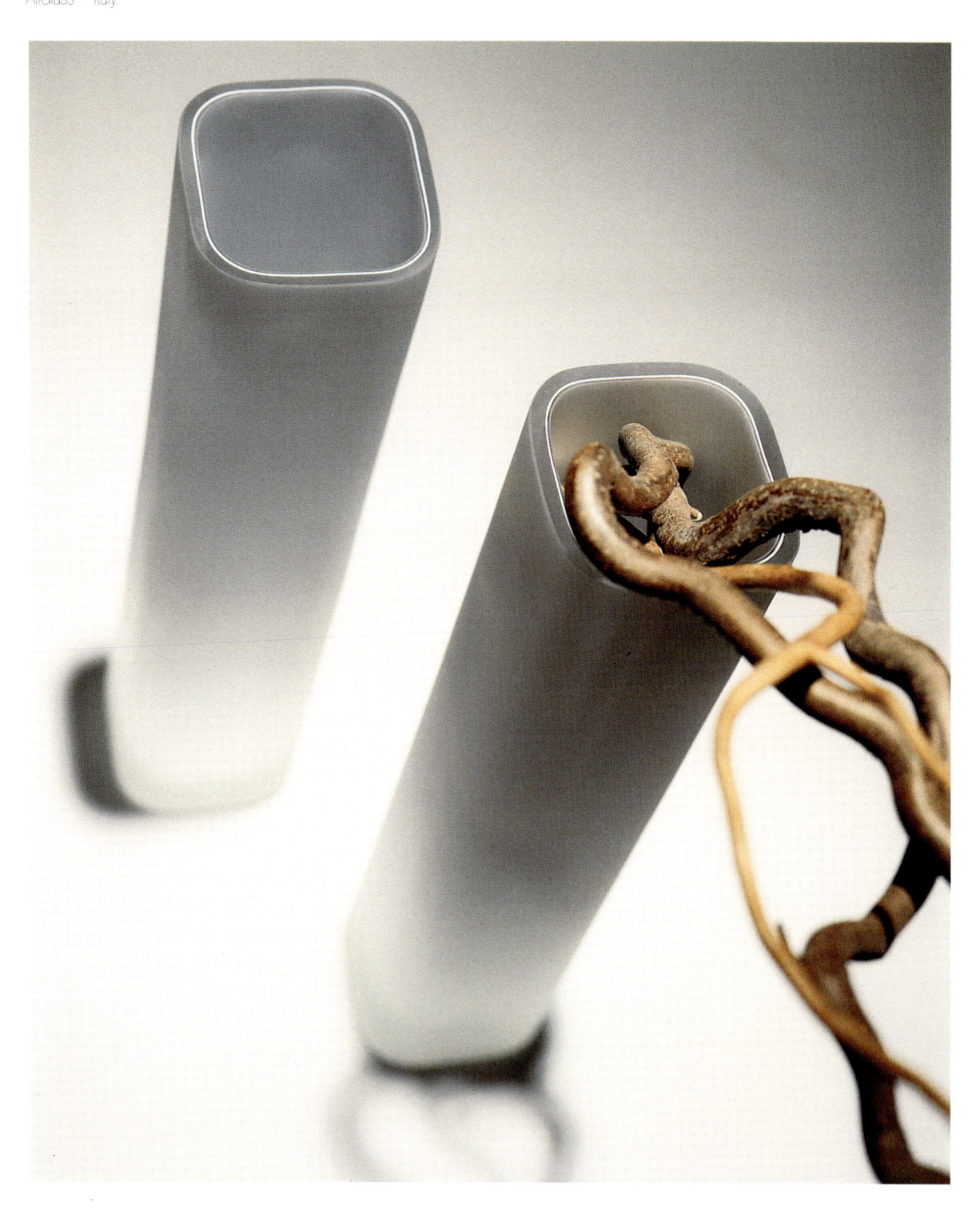

Constantin and Laurene Boym
Vases – American Plumbing
PVC
h 38cm – di 9cm
h 15in – di 3½in
Boym Design Studio – USA
prototype

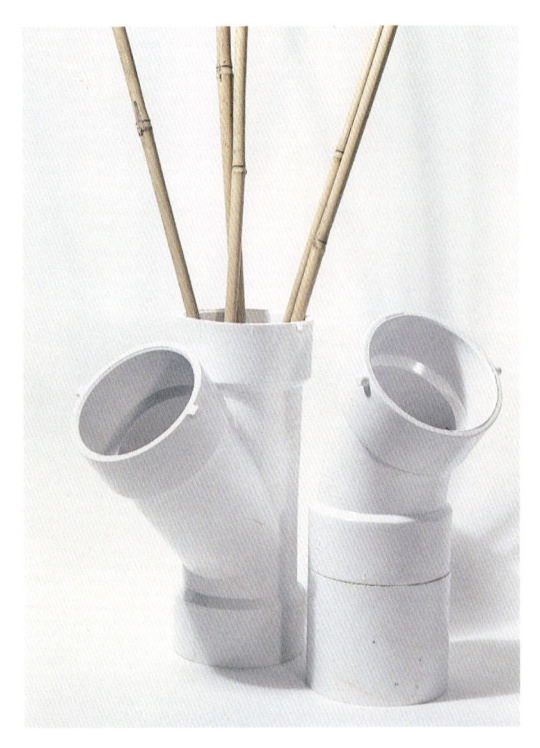

Marcel Wanders
Sponge Vase
porcelain – sponge
h max. 10cm – di 20cm
h max. 3⅞in – di 7⅞in
Wanders Wonders – The Netherlands

These vases are yet another statement in the continuing story of the (mis?) appropriation of forms from one universe of use and their arrival in a parallel universe where their very ordinariness renders them quirky. At best objects such as these attain the status of commentators on our pre-occupations with form, decoration and value. The use of workaday formal languages to make objects of luxury contains a critique of both our value systems and the lexicon of forms developed by designers. In their appearance out of their normal context, such forms cannot help but be divertingly decorative, if only for a short time. At worst, such forms become, over time, ill-advised jokes made against a backdrop of serious endeavour. – MH

Tableware

Marcel Wanders
Eggshell Vase
porcelain
h max. 20cm – d 15cm
h max. 7 7/8 in – d 5 7/8 in
Wanders Wonders – The Netherlands

Ronan Bouroullec
Vases Combinatoires
plastic
h 4–19.5cm – w 10.5cm – l 10.5–38cm – di 3.3–12.2cm
h 1⅝–7⅝in – w 4⅛in – l 4⅛–15in – di 1¼–4¾in
Néotù – France

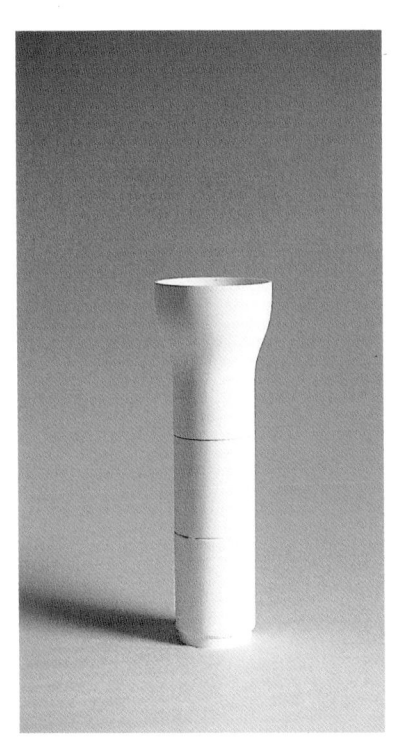

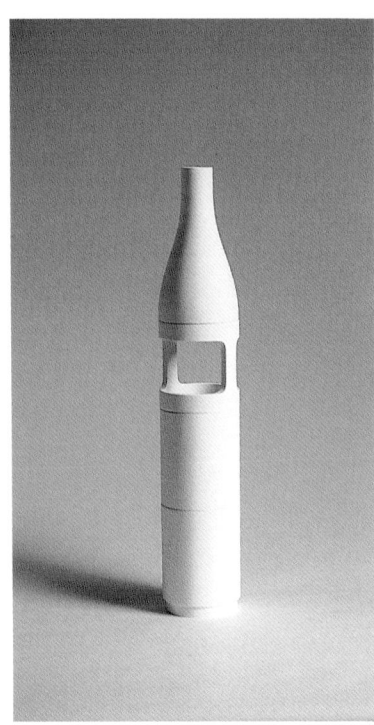

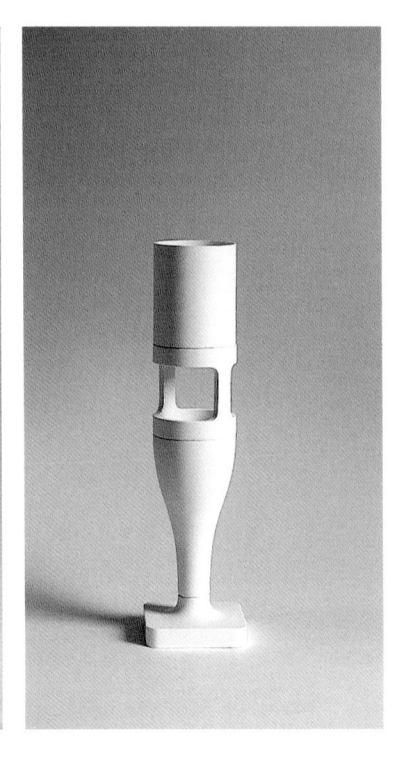

Tableware

116

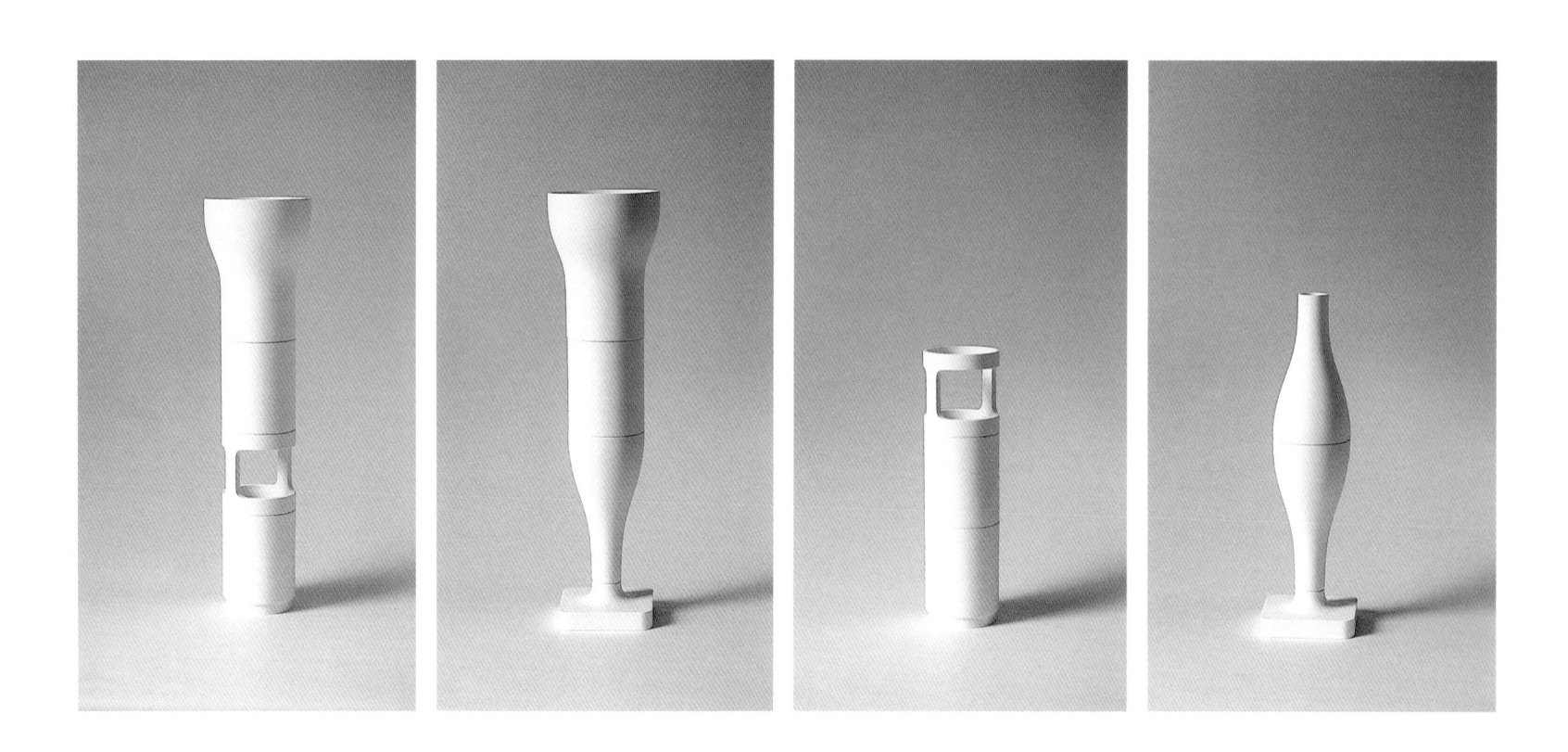

Tableware

Hella Jongerius
B-Service
porcelain – chamotte clay
h 2–35cm – di 3.5–35cm
h ¾–13¾in – di 1⅜–13¾in
DMD – The Netherlands

Tableware

Kazuhiko Tomita
Kazuhiko Collection – Morode
porcelain
salad bowl – h 11cm – di 23cm
   h 4³⁄₈in – di 9in
large meat plate – h 3.2cm – di 31.5cm
   h 1¼in – di 12³⁄₈in
meat plate – h 3cm – di 25cm
   h 1¹⁄₈in – di 9⁷⁄₈in
pasta dish – h 4cm – di 20cm
   h 1⁵⁄₈in – di 7⁷⁄₈in
Covo – Italy

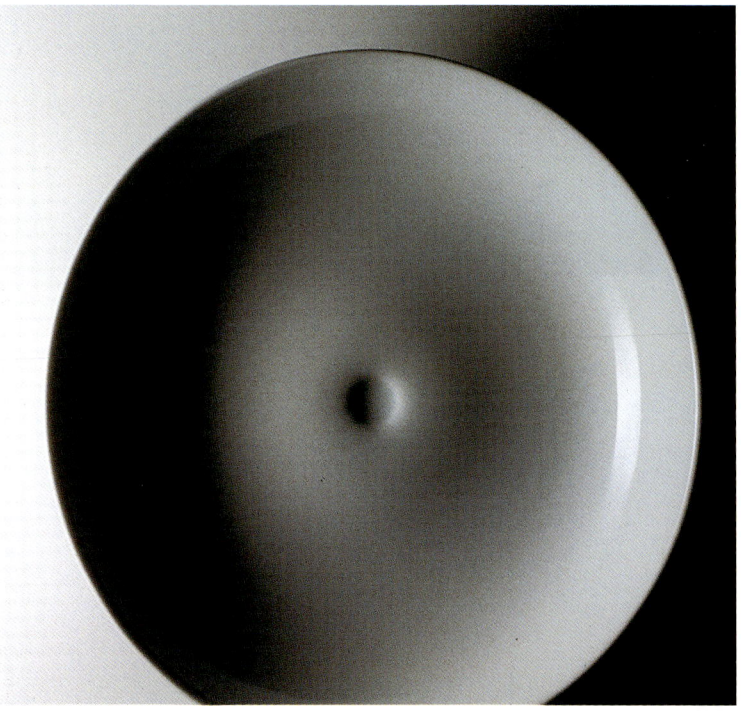

Katsuhiko Ogino
Tableware – Project-21
porcelain
h 4cm/4.5cm/5cm – di 12cm/17cm/22cm
h 1⅝in/1¾in/2in – di 4¾in/6⅝in/8⅝in

Tableware

Marcel Wanders
Foam Bowl
porcelain – foam
h max. 7cm – di 25cm
h max. 2 ¾in – di 9 ⅞in
Wanders Wonders – The Netherlands

Dick van Hoff
Extrusion Plates
porcelain
h 2cm – di 28cm
h ¾in – di 11in
DMD – The Netherlands for Rosenthal – Germany

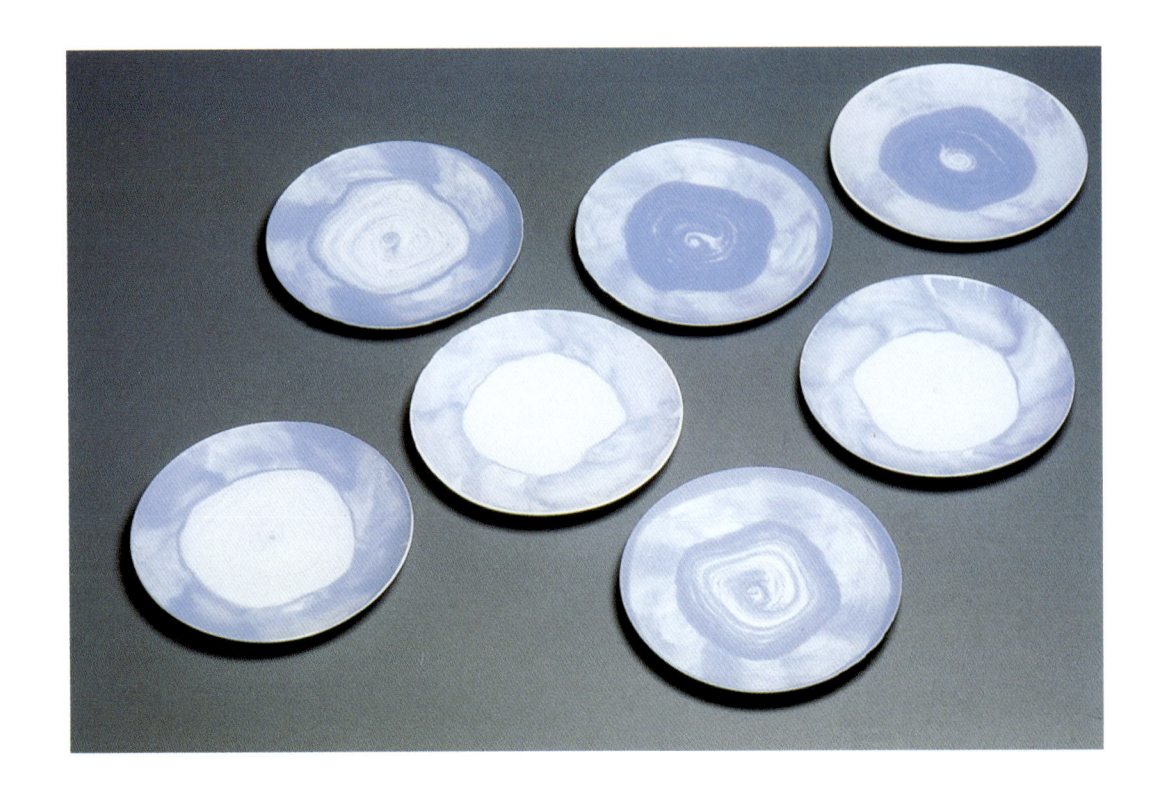

Tableware

Kazuhiko Tomita
Centrepiece – Atabow
stoneware
h 4cm – di 38cm
h 1 5/8in – di 15in
Laboratorio Pesaro – Italy
limited batch production

The appearance of something as anachronistic and atavistic as a stoneware centrepiece implies that somewhere in the world the experience of dining remains firmly lodged in the practices of the nineteenth century. The dressing of a formal table with a central focus implies dining on a scale which is foreign to most people outside of restaurants. On a domestic level, such a piece is ostentatious. The piece itself is visually and formally interesting, but the use for which it is designed means it can never be more than a short-run exercise in formal exactitude, and of course there is value in that. – MH

Emmanuel Babled
Table Service/Gift Objects
porcelain
vase – h 18cm/25cm/36cm – di 13.5cm/19.5cm/16cm
    h 7in/9⅞in/14⅛in – di 5⅜in/7¾in/6¼in
bowl – h 7cm/16.5cm – di 15cm/31cm
    h 2¾in/6½in – di 5⅛in/12¼in
Rosenthal – Germany
prototype

Tableware

Ronan Bouroullec
Coffee Cup – No. 4
porcelain
h 6.6cm – w 7cm – l 12cm
h 2⅝in – w 2¾in – l 4¾in
Evans & Wong – France

Some of the most rigorous executions are in the design of airline food containers. It is interesting to see that language bleeding from the disposable and ephemeral into the more solid and cherished world of porcelain. The coffee cup – long modelled on the tea cup – deserves its own morphology. Perhaps this is it. – MH

Enzo Mari
Two-dish Fruitstand – EM04
PP – stainless steel
h 20cm – di 19cm
h 7⅞in – di 7½in
Alessi – Italy

Ronan Bouroullec
Vase
ceramic
h 4.5cm – w 33cm – l 33cm
h 1¾in – w 13in – l 13in
Cappellini – Italy

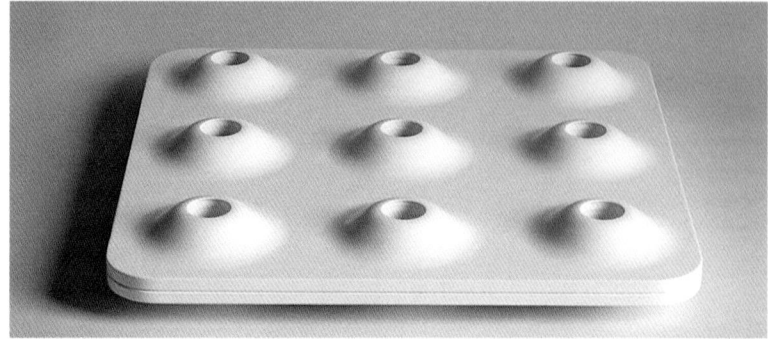

Tableware

Ronan Bouroullec
Wall-mounted Vase
ceramic – wood – aluminium
h 35cm – w 8cm – d 10cm
h 13¾in – w 3⅛in – d 3⅞in
Ligne Roset – France

Vessels continue to mutate their form beyond expectation. Notable here is the Bouroullec vase which is closer to a propagation tray than any traditional take on one of the implements of flower arranging. The wall-hung vase is also an interesting development as traditional vases usually depend upon a surface designed for display to have maximum domestic effect. Now, in these times of straightened domestic circumstances where space is continually at a premium, the wall can be a display surface for vessels which usually demand the horizontal in order to do their jobs. – MH

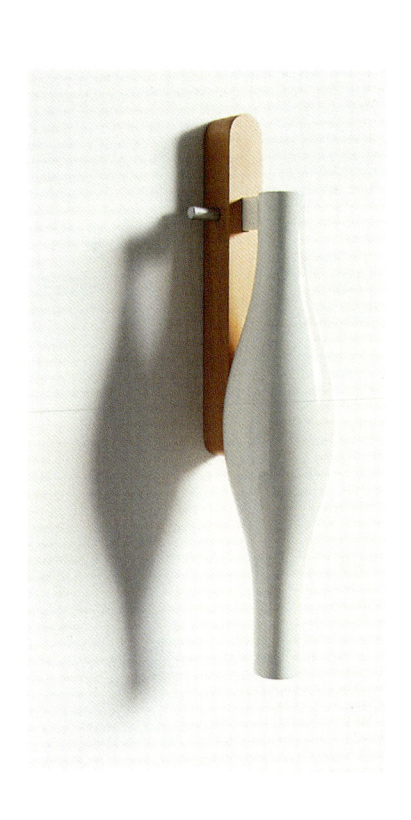

Arnout Visser and Erik Jan Kwakkel
Double-walled Tumblers and Cooler
porcelain
tumbler – h 9cm – di 4cm
h 3½in – di 1½in
cooler – h 30cm – di 15cm
h 11⅞in – di 5⅞in
DMD – The Netherlands
prototype

The disposable polystyrene cup is a staple object which has become a ubiquitous part of the throwaway ethic of fast food and machine-vended comestibles. The strength of the object lies in its light weight combined with high insulating properties which allow the cup to be held whilst full of scalding liquid. A by-product of the petroleum industry, it is a low cost and environmentally impactful product. In Visser and Kwakkel's take on the cup, the disposable becomes permanent and the form, rather than being a simple jokey lift from the world of the ordinary into the special, replicates the ergonomically perfect design complete with carrying rim and couples it with a double skin of porcelain to retain the form's traditional cool-to-the-touch properties. – MH

Tableware

Gijs Bakker
Teapot – Knitted Maria
porcelain
h 28cm – di 28cm
h 11in – di 11in
Droog Design – The Netherlands
for Rosenthal – Germany

Masatoshi Sakaegi
Mug from the Common Series
melamine
h 8.9cm – di 7.9cm
h 3½in – di 3½in
Kokusai Kako Co. – Japan

Mark Garside
CD/Letter/Toast Holder – Digital Grass
PVC
h 10cm – w 14cm – d 14cm
h 3⅞in – w 5½in – d 5½in
Inflate – UK

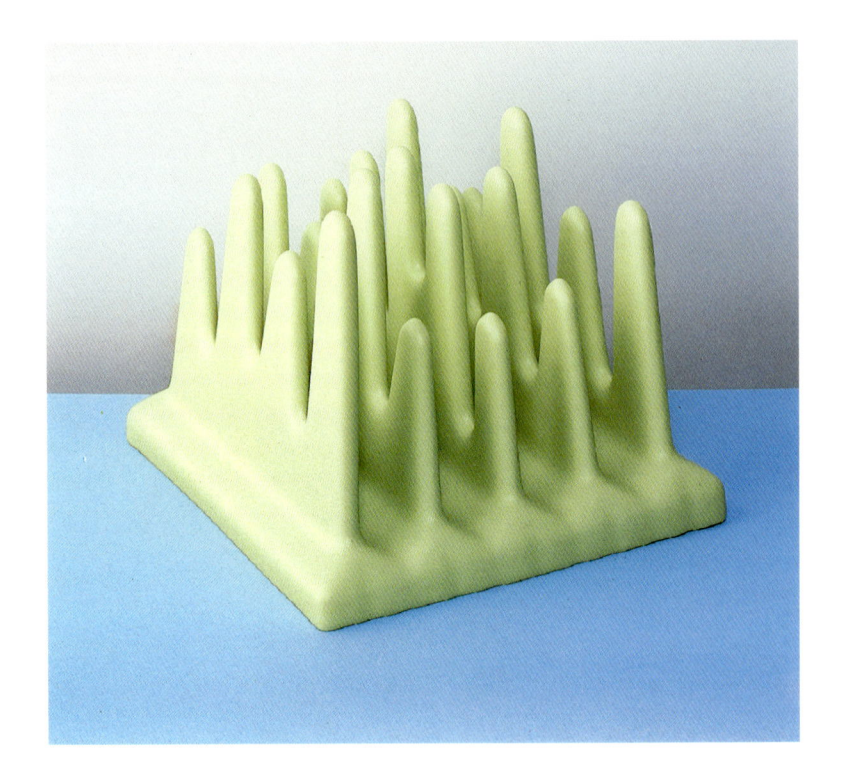

Tableware

Stefano Giovannoni
Spice Containers – Happy Spices
PMMA – PE – polyamide
h 11.5cm – di 6.8cm
h 4½in – di 2¾in
Alessi – Italy

Marc Newson
Dishrack – Dish Doctor
injection-moulded plastic
h 10.4cm – w 46cm – d 39cm
h 4in – w 18⅛in – d 15⅜in
Magis – Italy

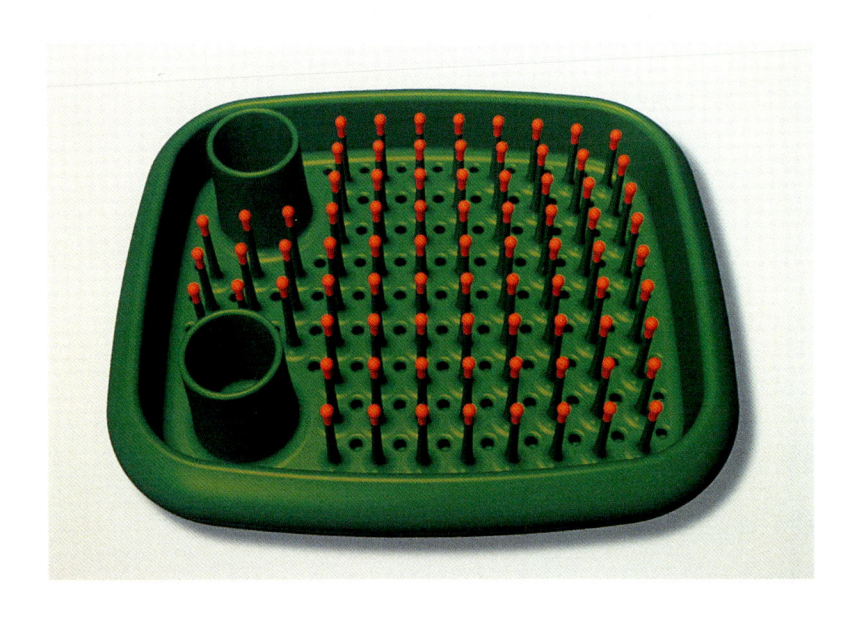

Aldo Rossi
Pitcher – AR01
stainless steel
h 21cm – di 12cm
h 8¼in – di 4½in
Alessi – Italy

Michael Young
Vase – MY 69
sterling silver
h 20cm – l 21cm – d 13cm
h 7⅞in – l 8¼in – d 5⅛in
Sawaya & Moroni – Italy
limited batch production

Tableware

Massimo Zucchi
Bread Dish and Centrepiece – Graph and Paragraph
sterling silver
Graph – h 2.5cm – di 30cm
    h 1in – di 11 7/8in
Paragraph – h 3.5cm – di 11cm
    h 1 3/8in – di 4 3/8in
Sawaya & Moroni – Italy
limited batch production

Björn Dahlström
Range of Casseroles and Pans – Dahlström 98
multi-layered stainless steel – aluminium – cast iron
casseroles – h 19cm/20cm – di 22cm/26cm
          h 7½in/7⅞in – di 8⅝in/10⅛in
Hackman Designor – Finland

Tableware

Range of Casseroles and Pans – Dahlström 98
multi-layered stainless steel – aluminium – cast iron
sauteuse – h 15.5cm – di 22cm
　　　　　h 6⅛in – di 8⅝in
saucepans – h 15.5cm/19.5cm – di 18cm/22cm
　　　　　h 6⅛in/7¾in – di 7in/8⅝in
sauté pan – di 32cm
　　　　　di 12⅝in
Hackman Designor – Finland

Range of Casseroles and Pans – Dahlström 98
multi-layered stainless steel – aluminium – cast iron
pot – h 20cm – di 28cm
   h 7⁷⁄₈in – di 11in
frying pans – h 4.5cm – di 26cm/32cm
   h 1¾in – di 10¼in/12⅝in
grillpan – h 3cm – di 26cm
   h 1¼in – di 10¼in
Hackman Designor – Finland

Tableware

Björn Dahlström has designed a range of cookware which covers all of the angles. Cooks will profess a preference for cooking with a particular material of a particular grade, but these pans manage to combine all of the traditional metalware cooking materials in one design. Having conquered the problem of differing coefficients of expansion, stainless steel, aluminium and cast iron are combined to make pans which must surely cater for all needs. – MH

Renzo Piano Workshop
Cutlery – Piano Workshop 98
stainless steel
fork – w 2.5cm – l 20cm
        w 1in – l 7⁷⁄₈in
knife – w 2cm – l 20.3cm
        w ¾in – l 8in
dessert spoon – w 3.4cm – l 20cm
        w 1³⁄₈in – l 7⁷⁄₈in
teaspoon – w 2.9cm – l 10.5cm
        w 1¹⁄₈in – l 4¹⁄₈in
Hackman Designor – Finland

Tableware

Antonio Citterio
Cutlery – Citterio con Löw 98
stainless steel
fork – w 2.5cm – l 19.3cm
  w 1in – l 7⅝in
knife – w 1.6cm – l 23cm
  w ⅝in – l 9in
spoon – w 4cm – l 19.3cm
  w 1⅝in – l 7⅝in
Hackman Designor – Finland

Stefan Lindfors
Salad Bowl and Servers – Lindfors 98
stainless steel
servers – w 9.5cm – l 30cm
w 3¾in – l 11⅞in
bowl – h 11cm – di 37.3cm
h 4⅜in – di 14⅝in
Hackman Designor – Finland

Tableware

Carina Seth-Andersson
Bowls and Servers – Seth-Andersson 98
wood – steel
servers – l 35cm
         l 13¾in
bowls – h 10cm/14cm – di 34cm/26cm
        h 4in/5½in – di 13⅜in/10¼in
Hackman Designor – Finland

Textiles

It was textile manufacture that kick-started the industrial revolution. Now traditional textile industries which weave in cotton and wool are having to contend and compete with textile industries which derive their raw materials from the petrochemical industries. Just what the word 'textile' means is increasingly open to definition. There are subsequently interesting anomalies in the world of textiles and fabrics. Carbon fibre is a textile before it is shaped and set to a form; Teflon – once the much vaunted derivative of the NASA space programme – can now be found in sports clothing. The upshot is that textile manufacture is no longer the sole domain of mill owners and landowners. Equally, the old hierarchies of materials from silk down to cotton, are undergoing significant change. New materials mean new uses, new uses mean a wider awareness of the material properties of what can only be called textiles. What those textiles are, however, is increasingly open to definition.

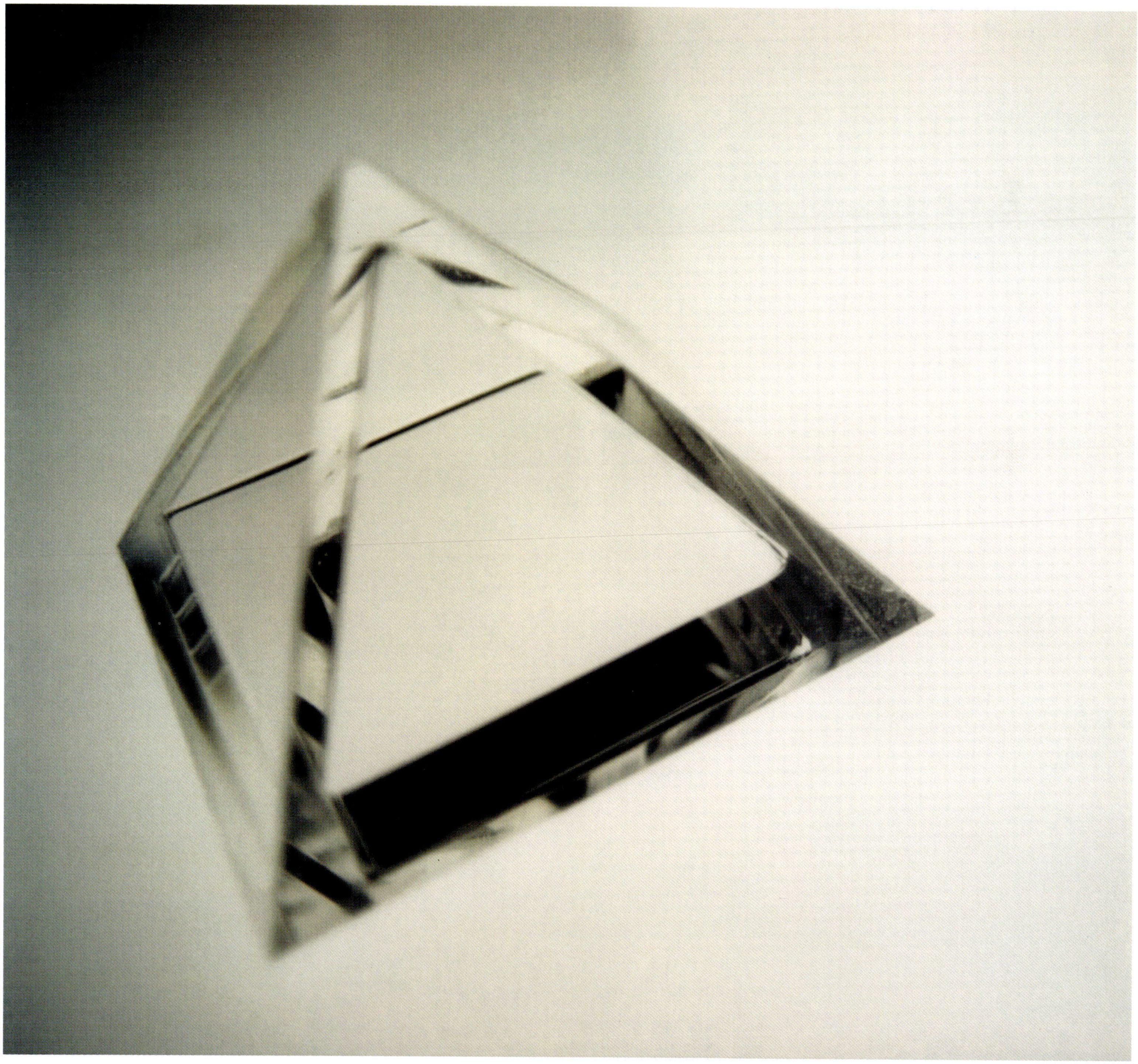

Eero Koivisto
Carpet – Golden Section
wool
w 200cm – l 200cm
w 78¾in – l 78¾in
Asplund – Sweden

Textiles

Vibeke Rohland
Room Divider – Peep Hole
industrial felt
h 270cm – w 186cm
h 106¼in – w 73¼in
limited batch production

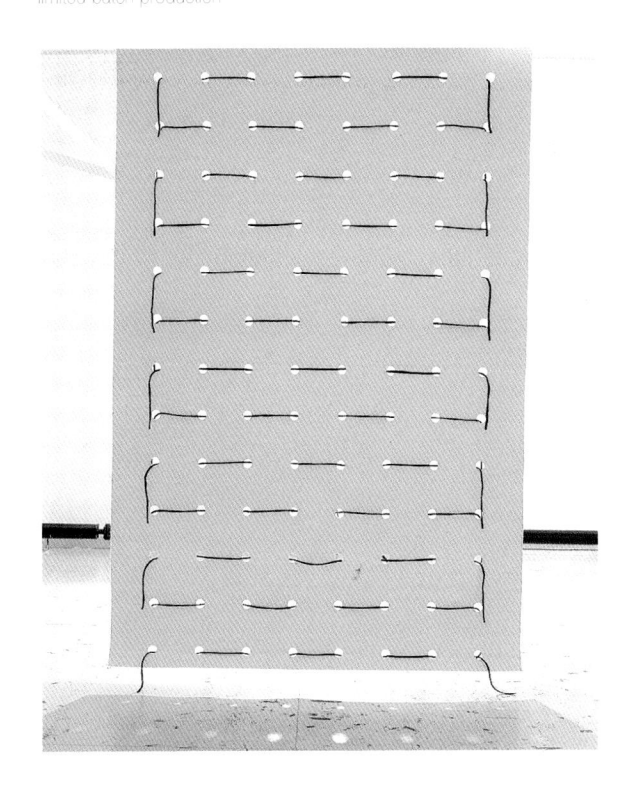

Debbie Jane Buchan
Computer-generated Surface Design – Blocks
Debbie Jane Buchan – UK

Textiles

Patrick Jouin
Carpet – Glup
wool – wood
w 180cm – l 240cm
w 70⅞in – l 94½in
Ligne Roset – France

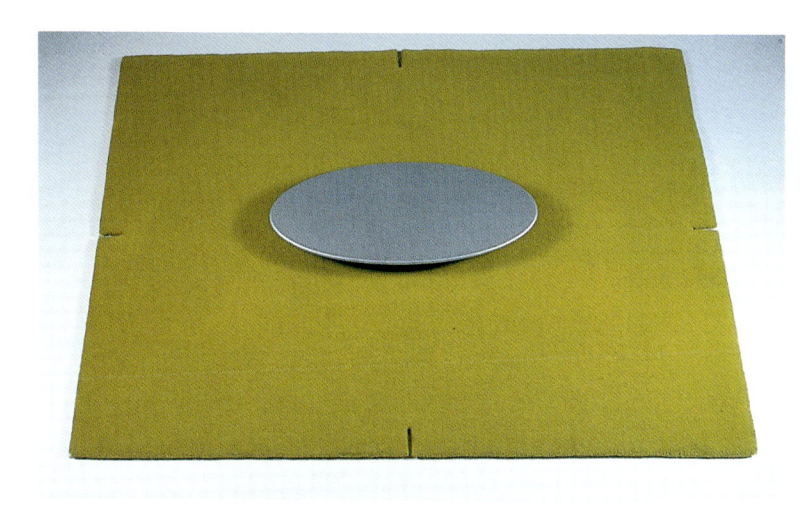

The invention of sculptural forms is the job of both the artist and the designer. Usually the task of inventing the pure form falls to the artist, the task of inventing the useful form falls to the designer. Taken in the abstract, an object like this could be said to bridge both areas. But design cannot live in the abstract. In use, this rug combines a traditional wool surface with what appears to be a handy table in the centre. This could be, if teamed with the rug as chair earlier in the book, the harbinger of a revolution in the way we use our floors. On the other hand it could be a useful invention for those of us who simply prefer to stretch out away from the constrictions and conventions imposed by plain old chairs. – MH

Matz Borgström
Carpet – O
wool
di 160cm
di 63in
Asplund – Sweden

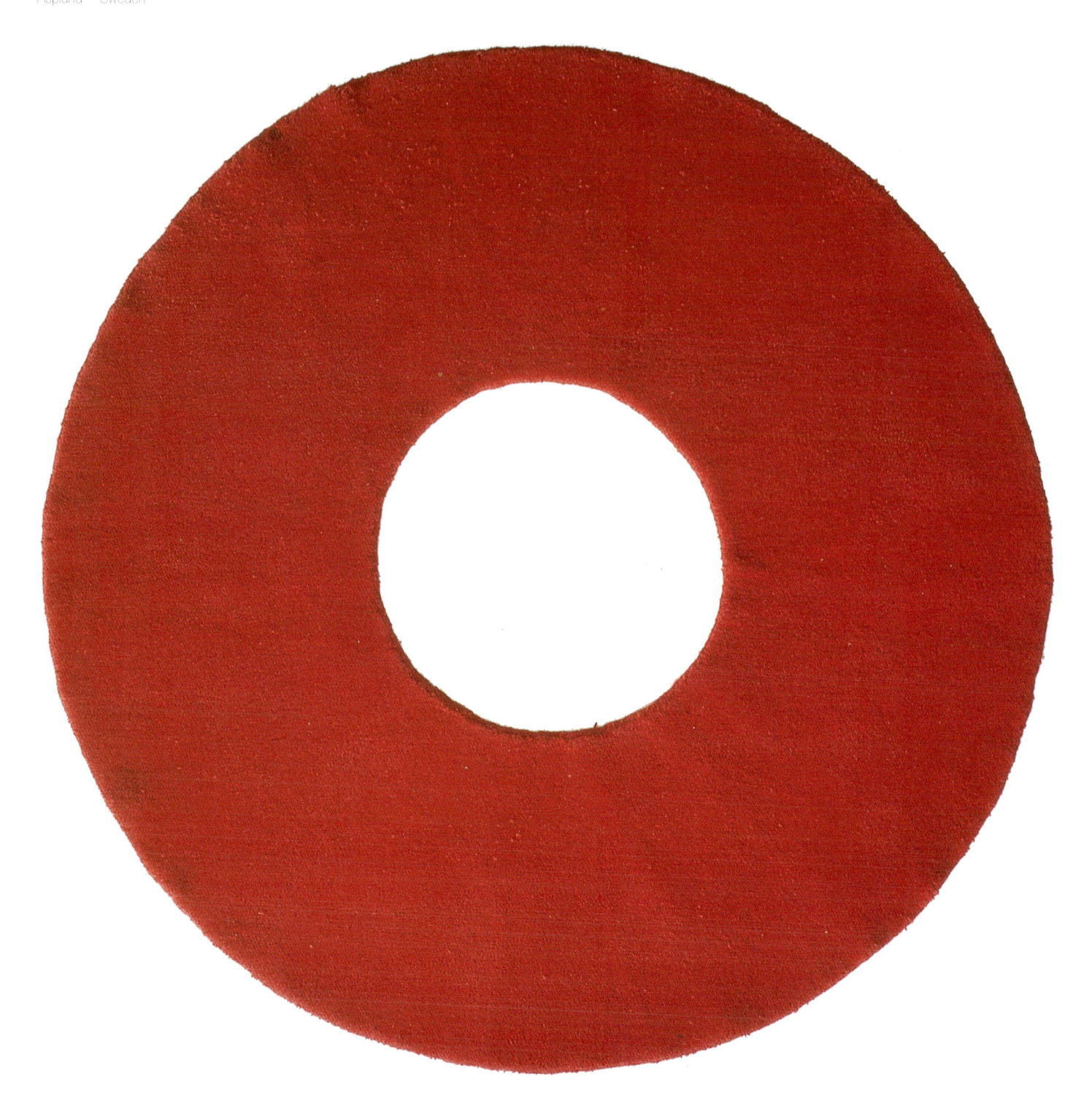

Textiles

Matz Borgström's rug is that rare hybrid of sculptural presence and decorative utility object. It is so simple in its conception that it is alone in this book in its approach to decoration and utility. — MH

Michael Sodeau
Carpet – Chris Cross
wool
w 200cm – l 130cm
w 78¾in – l 51⅛in
Asplund – Sweden

Because they offer a flat surface, designers usually approach rug design as they would a piece of paper and often the results are, as on this page, beguilingly modern and inevitably graphic. Rugs carry the essence of the mark made on paper, transferred through machinery to the foam-sealed hessian medium of the rug, in a way that other three-dimensional products can never do. At their best, rugs offer their buyers the chance to live with a well-rendered decorative graphic. At their worst they are the carriers of the worst kind of illustrative excess. The rugs depicted here are in the former category, although it should be said that there are not enough rugs exploring the three-dimensional effects attainable with their surfaces and form. – MH

Textiles

James Irvine
Carpet - x5
wool
w 200cm – l 250cm
w 78¾in – l 98⅜in
Asplund - Sweden

Lloyd Schwan
Carpets – Ruggles
wool
w 60–180cm – l 60–180cm
w 23⅝–70⅞in – l 23⅝–70⅞in
Asplund – Sweden

Textiles

Michael Sodeau
Rug – George
wool
w 121cm – l 183cm
w 48in – l 72in
Michael Sodeau Partnership – UK
limited batch production

Textiles

Pia Wallén
Carpet – Dot
wool
made to order
Asplund – Sweden

Pia Wallén
Carpet – Krux
wool
w 120cm – l 120cm
w 47 ¼in – l 47 ¼in
Asplund – Sweden

Textiles

Tom Dixon
Carpet – Maze
wool
w 200cm – 1200cm
w 78¾in – 178¾in
Asplund – Sweden

Ronan Bouroullec
Rug/Carpet – Moquette
acrylic
rug – w 50cm – l 50cm
w 19⅝in – l 19⅝in
Sommer – France
prototype

Textiles

Reiko Sudo
Fabric – Wavelets
polyester – nylon – paper – polyurethane
w 90cm
w 35⅜in
Nuno Corporation – Japan

Textiles

Fabric — Patched Paper
polyester — paper
w 112cm
w 44in
Nuno Corporation — Japan

Reiko Sudo
Fabric – Delphos Pleats
polyester
w 140cm
w 55⅛in
Nuno Corporation – Japan

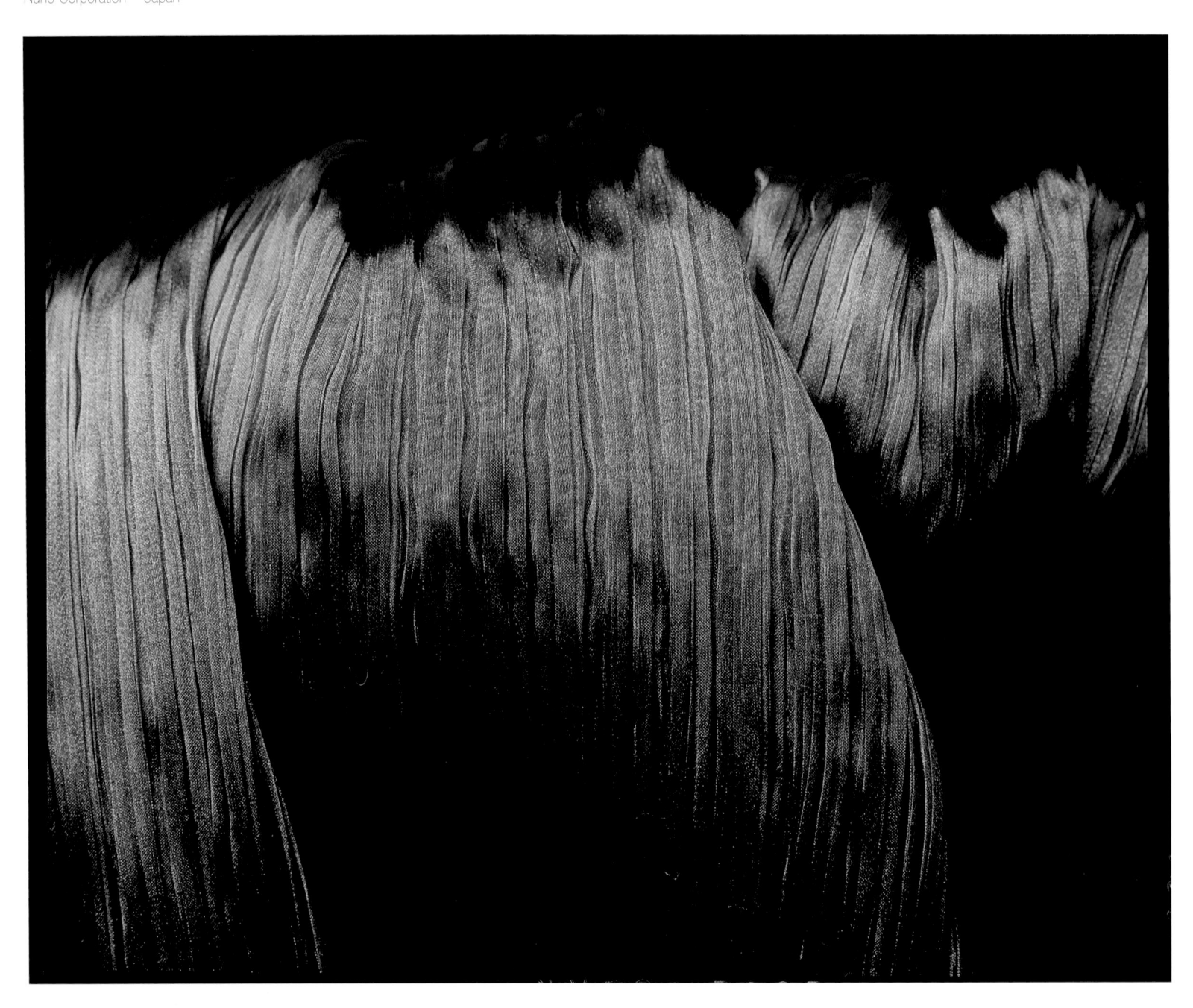

Textiles

Fabric — Otterskin
polyester
w 140cm
w 55 ⅛in
Nuno Corporation — Japan

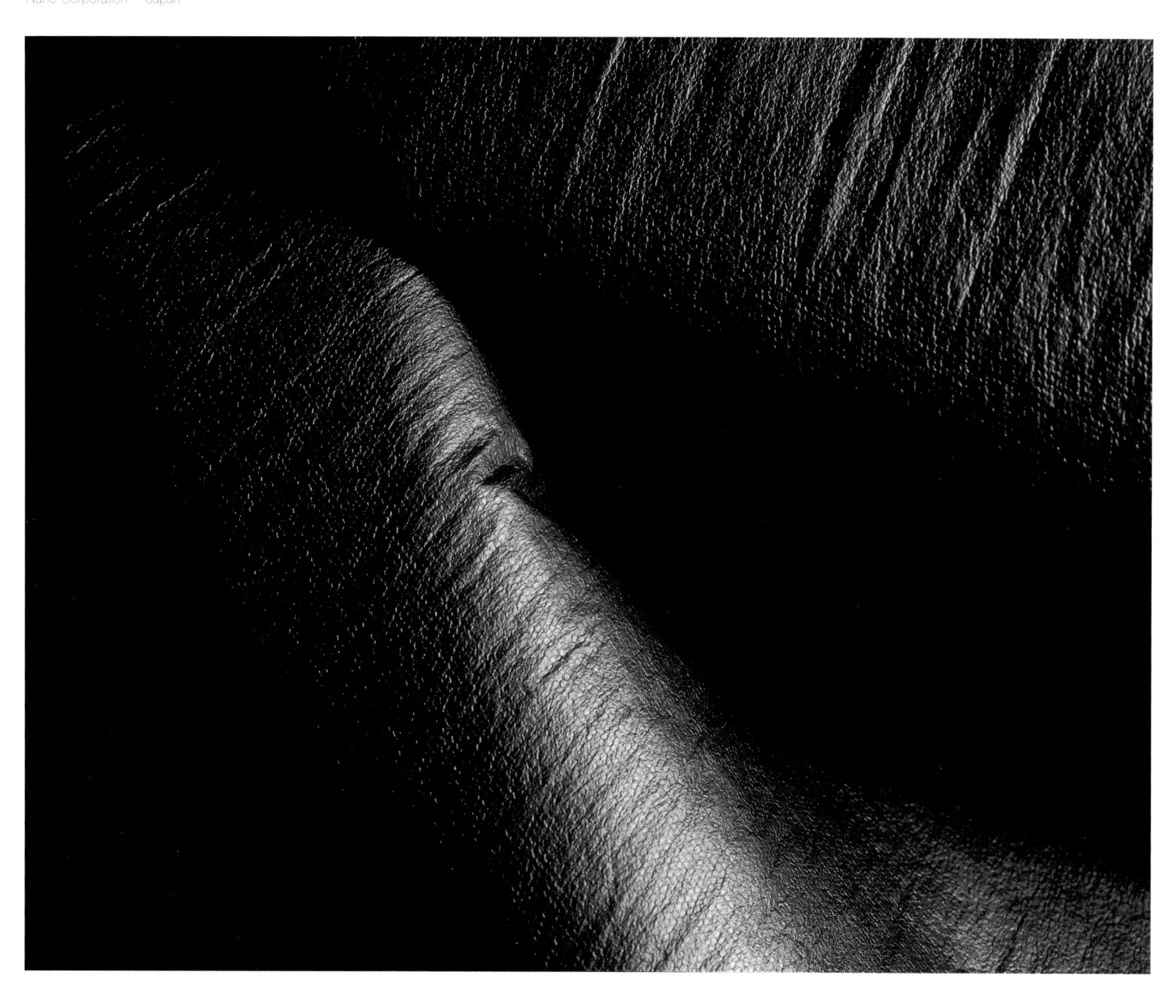

Eugène van Veldhoven
Shower Curtain
cotton — silicone rubber
w 120cm
w 47 1/4 in
prototype

Textiles

Timorous Beasties
Fabric – Funky Pallette
cotton
w 60cm – l 136cm
w 23⅝in – l 53½in
Timorous Beasties – UK

Textiles

Masako Hayashibe
Tapestry – Laboratorium
nylon thread
h 180cm – di 22cm
h 70⅞in – di 8⅝in
one-off

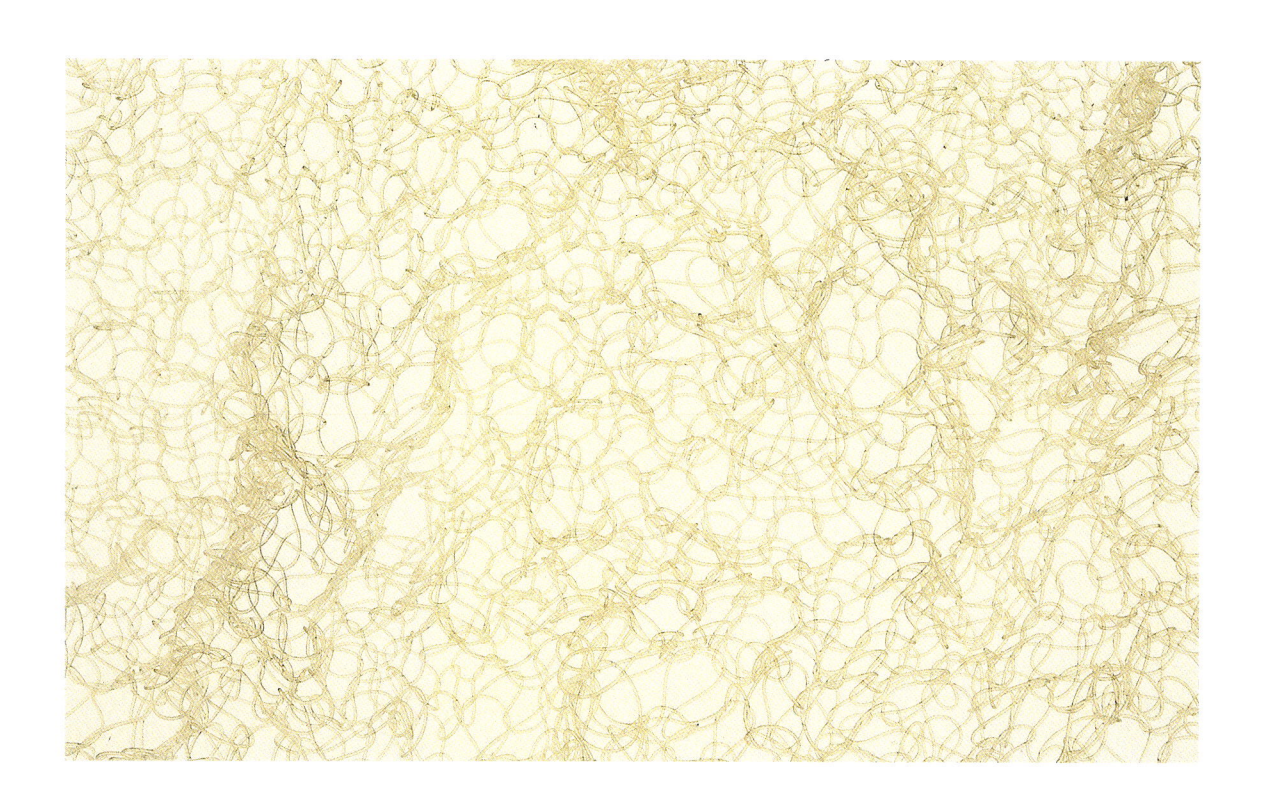

Barbara Brenner
Decorating Fabric – Circus
30% cotton – 70% polyester
w 300cm
w 118 1/8 in
Nya Nordiska – Germany

Decorating Fabric – Palme
cotton
w 140cm
w 55 1/8 in
Nya Nordiska – Germany

Textiles

Bute Design Studio
Range of Upholstery Fabric
wool
various sizes
Bute – UK

Products

Product design has the potential to change the way we live, and perhaps more importantly, to change the way we think we live. By wrapping complex technologies in housings that speak to us of the object's function, and that also speak to us of the aspirations of the owners, designers are able to offer us the possibility of feeling that we are achieving happiness and therefore satisfaction through the things we consume. But at the bottom line, it is the way things work and look that determines the degree of affection we feel for them. In order that the product itself should not get in the way of this direct communication of the idea of the product, a new rule is emerging – the more complex the technology we are asked to buy, the more simple the interface between us and that technology seems to become. The apogee of this state is seen in the computer which is simply taken from the box and plugged in. The computer then works. Every complex function of this complex machine is masked behind the primary layer of functional style afforded the machine by the product designer. This is its selling point. On the other hand, MiniDisc players and DVD decks come bristling with the same kind of multifunctioning displays that characterized the early stereo music centres. Their evolution into one-touch systems cannot be far away.

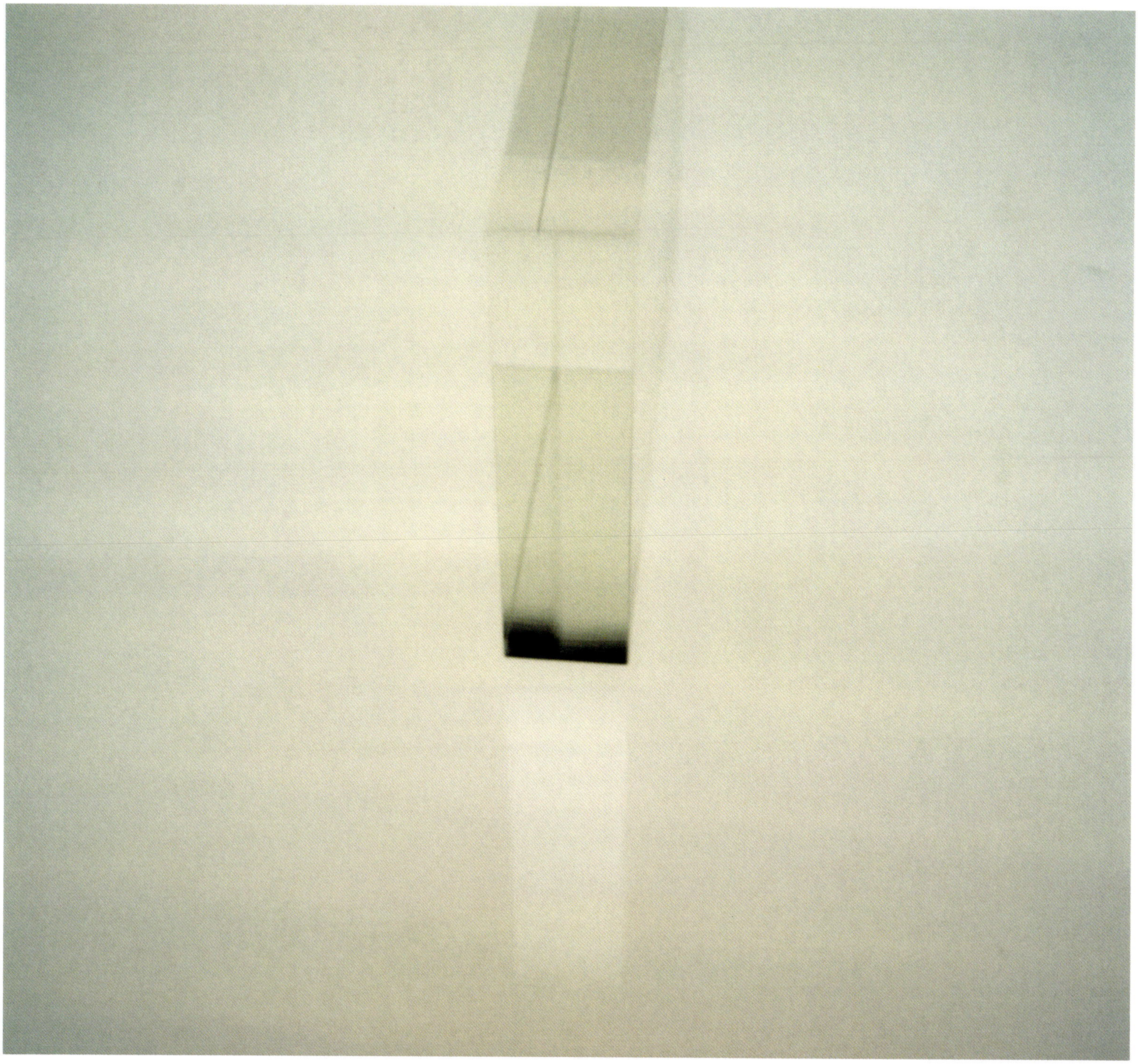

Thomas Meyerhöffer
Portable Computer – Apple eMate
plastic – polycarbonate
h 5.3cm – w 30.5cm – d 29cm
h 2in – w 12in – d 11³⁄₈in
Apple Computer – USA

Products

For those interested in our relationship with the cyberworld, Apple represents the kind of computer company that has long been in opposition to the 'bigger' organizations like IBM and, latterly, Microsoft. Purveyors of hardware rather than software, Apple invented the E-mate as the first attempt at re-positioning themselves as the one computer company that made everything easy in a human way. Design has clearly played a big part in the re-invention of the marque as the modern must-have. The E-mate was specifically designed for schoolchildren to carry with them and features easy word-processing software and a range of other features akin to Mum and Dad's Mac machine back home. Formally speaking, it's an interesting phenomenon when portable computers, usually perceived as hard-edged business tools, are transformed into candy-coloured, child-friendly accessories that are web and e-mail prepped and ready to go. This may be the first manifestation of an altruistic and egalitarian way forward for an increasingly digitally literate younger generation, made possible by Apple Macintosh. On the other hand, the E-mate could be seen as the first manifestation of a strongly jesuit approach to marketing and design. Give me the child until he is seven, this machine seems to imply, and I will give you the man. – MH

Sam Hecht/IDEO Japan
Desktop Computer — Whitebox
methacrylate — ABS plastic
h 32cm — w 10cm — d 25cm
h 12 5/8in — w 3 7/8in — d 9 7/8in
NEC Corporation — Japan
prototype

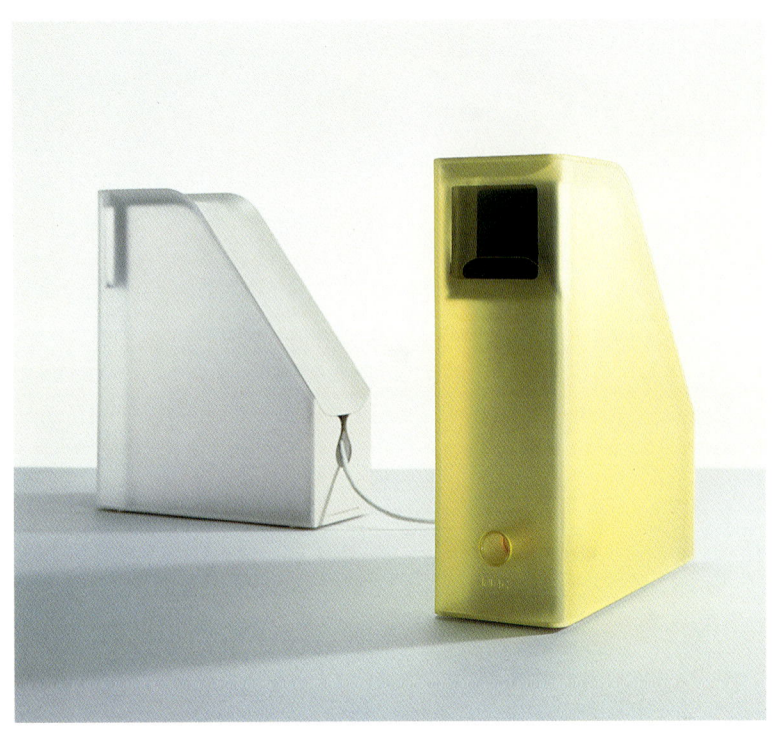

The computer's domestic life and presence is continually changing as the needs and aspirations of those who work on computers at home determine the object's form. We are only too used to the faceless grey box that sits in the corner with its unfathomable whirrings, clicks and squelches letting us know it is working. Unfortunately the visual syntaxes of the computer room in a corporation do not necessarily lend themselves to the domestic sphere. The result is that the need or the desire to work at home has led to the incursion of an industrial aesthetic into our living spaces which is quite at odds with the way that many people wish to relate to technology in their homes. Enter the computer in a different box. The magazine/file storage box is a staple of any office, and clearly the thinking here is inspired by the idea of camouflage. A hard disk concealed in a box like any other to be found in the home office is a justifiably neat idea which, for all but product display fetishists, represents a degree of liberation from the family of boxes (computers, stereos, televisions) which refuse to live anywhere other than in the spaces in the home that they define and then dominate. Mercifully this solution stops well short of the school of thought which conceals technology within Queen Anne commodes. — MH

Products

Naoto Fukasawa/IDEO Japan
Computer – Whitebox
ABS plastic
h 100cm – w 32.5cm – d 19cm
h 39 ³⁄₈in – w 12 ³⁄₄in – d 7 ½in
NEC Corporation – Japan
prototype

Naoto Fukasawa/IDEO Japan
Home Colour Printer – Printables
ABS plastic – metal wire
h 100cm – w 48cm – d 30cm
h 39³⁄₈in – w 18⁷⁄₈in – d 11⁷⁄₈in
Epson – Japan
one-off

Products

Sam Hecht/IDEO Japan
Home Colour Printer – Printables
methacrylate – ABS plastic
h 24cm – w 46cm – d 23.5cm
h 9³⁄₈in – w 18⅛in – d 9¼in
Epson – Japan
one-off

Computer peripherals – printers, scanners and disk drives – are traditionally made to resemble scions of their grey-faced parents. But there are mainstream moves afoot to change the way in which computers define themselves on the desktop at home. The recent launch of the Apple iMac is evidence enough of this, as are the peripherals on these pages which in their cool simplicity and muted colours and forms resemble no less than a new breed of friendly domestic machinery. The relationship of these machines to the traditional computer box is made physically through the connecting cable. Visually, there is little connection at all. This is a situation which is to be applauded, even if the formal languages in these examples are reliant on the naively beguiling appeal of the new. – MH

Motomi Kawakami
42in Plasma-Monitor and Television – PX-42V2/PX-42MZ
aluminium – plastic
h 64.8cm – w 104.8cm – d 8.9cm
h 25½in – w 41¼in – d 3½in
NEC Corporation – Japan

Notwithstanding the comments on previous pages about the uncompromising nature of technology's presence in the home, there are exceptions which have to be made when a piece of equipment of staggeringly grandiose technological prowess hoves into view. The flat screen technology which drives this enormous 'boy's toy' has been in development for many years; the theory is that a flat picture delivered in this proportion is easier for the brain to read as an image. It certainly seems to work as flat screens deliver a sharper, more consistent, colour correct picture. There is, as ever, the issue of size to contend with. Such screens are probably unsuitable for anything other than the mythical modern loft space. – MH

Products

Yoshinori Yamada and John Tree
Wide and Flat Screen TV – KV-32FD1
plastic
h 56.1cm – w 84.6cm – d 55.5cm
h 22 1/8in – w 33 3/8in – d 21 7/8in
Sony Corp. – Japan

Naoto Fukasawa/IDEO Japan
Monitor – NEC Multisync
ABS plastic
h 44cm – w 36.5cm – d 40.6cm
h 17 3/8in – w 14 3/8in – d 16in
NEC America/Packard Bell – USA

Products

Design Centre/AV Systems Group/Sharp Corporation
LCD Display TV – LC-150F1/LC-121F1
ABS plastic
h 30.9cm – w 35.7cm – d 8.7cm
h 12 1/8in – w 14in – d 3 1/2in
Sharp Corporation – Japan

A trip to the electrical retail district of Tokyo would reveal a plethora of such screens on offer to the public at discount prices. Not only are these screens based upon LCD technology, the crucial difference which allows them to be flatter and more minimal than their predecessors, but they are also only available in NTSC configuration, a fact which makes them tantalizingly unavailable to those in the West who would appreciate and welcome such slim and unobstrusive inhabitants into their homes. – MH

Design Centre/AV Systems Group/Sharp Corporation in collaboration with Porsche Design GmbH
Digital ViewCam – VL-EF1
ABS plastic – magnesium alloy
h 9.3cm – w 16.2cm – d 5.6cm
h 3⅝in – w 6⅜in – d 2¼in
Sharp Corporation – Japan

The small digital video camera is busily transforming people's relationship to video and the camcorder. The idea that the camera can be carried around easily and deployed at will without drawing attention to itself simply makes it easier to record our everyday lives. With the coming proliferation of television channels it is likely that such technology will be used to fill up the available space which will be increasing exponentially. – MH

Products

Design Centre/Information Systems Group/Sharp Corporation
Power Personal Information Tool – MI-506DC
ABS plastic
h 2.3cm – w 16.1cm – d 9cm
h 7/8in – w 6 3/8in – d 3 1/2in
Sharp Corporation – Japan

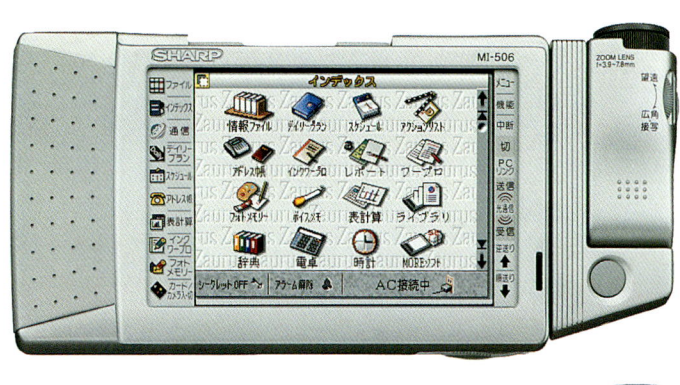

Shin Miyashita
Digital Mavica – MVC-FD7
plastic
h 11cm – w 12.7cm – d 7.3cm
h 4 3/8in – w 5in – d 2 7/8in
Sony Corp. – Japan

The function of the digital camera as a recorder is clear, but design is creeping into the equation to move the digital camera away from its pure function towards that of the fashionable accessory. The miniaturization of the camera is one of the truly telling contributions to the visual culture and hence the visual literacy of the late twentieth century. – MH

Products

Design Centre/AV Systems Group/Sharp Corporation
LCD Digital Still Camera – VE-LC2
h 6.1cm – w 10.8cm – d 3.1cm
h 2⅜in – w 4¼in – d 1¼in
Sharp Corporation – Japan

Kaoru Sumita
Digital Handycam – DCR-PC10
die-cast magnesium
h 12.9cm – w 6.1cm – l 11.8cm
h 5in – w 2⅜in – l 4⅝in
Sony Corp. – Japan

Matsushita Electric Industrial Co. Ltd
Portable DVD Player – DVD-L10
ABS plastic
h 4.3cm – w 16cm – d 16cm
h 1¾in – w 6¼in – d 6¼in
Matsushita Electric Industrial Co. – Japan

Products

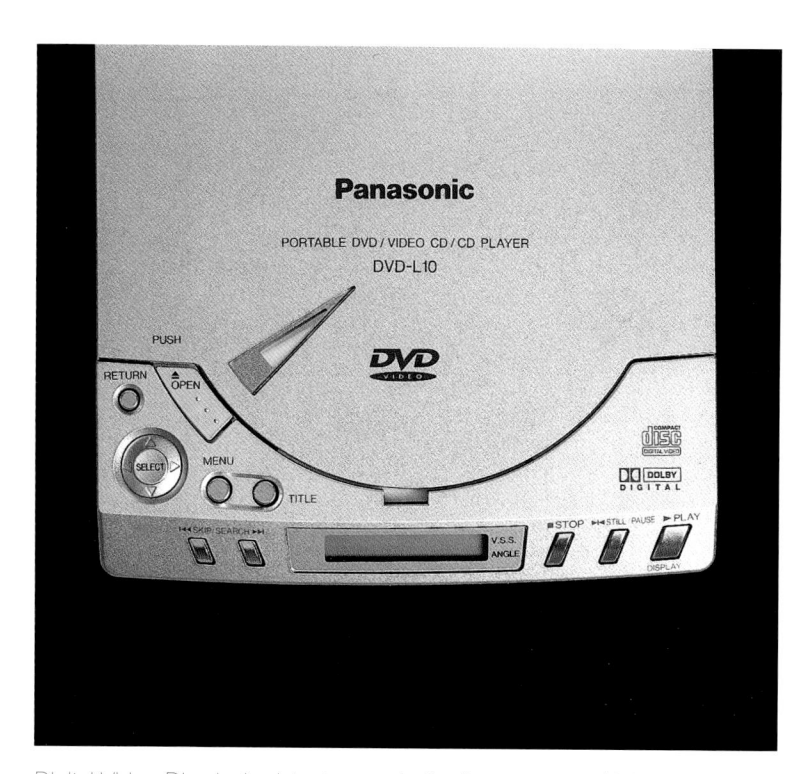

Digital Video Disc is the latest move in the format wars which started with the battle between Betamax and VHS. Now, the search for consumer friendly formats has pushed the continuous technological leapfrogging to the extent where a high-resolution video format has come into being which can be carried anywhere. This kind of equipment points the way to a world wherein a fully writable digital format will allow personal soundtracks and visuals to be carried anywhere. – MH

Masakazu Kanatani
Portable MiniDisc player – MZ-E35
die-cast magnesium – compressed aluminium
h 1.9cm – w 8.2cm – l 8cm
h ³⁄₄in – w 3¹⁄₄in – l 3¹⁄₈in
Sony Corporation – Japan

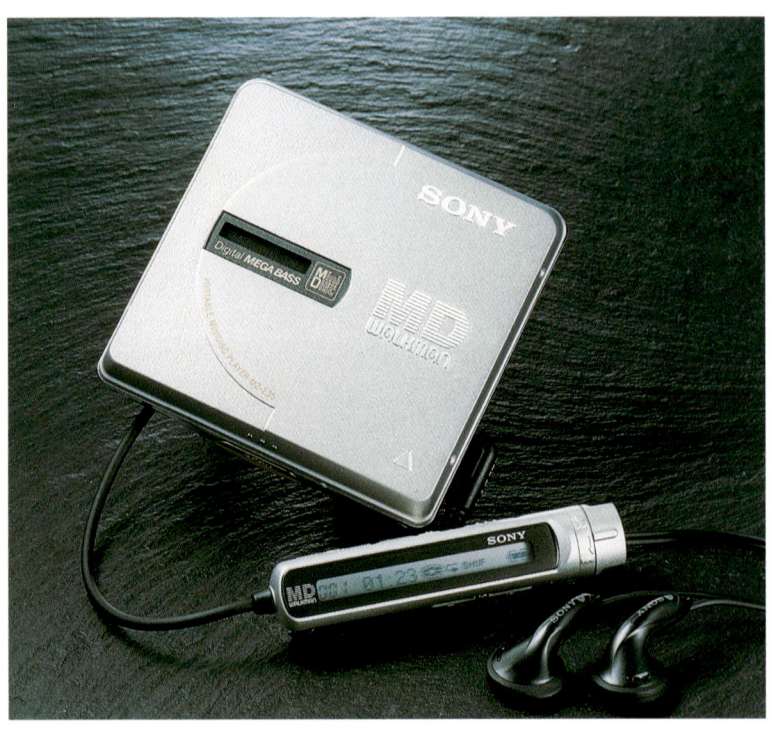

The portable, fully writable aural format is already here in the shape of the MiniDisc which allows the transfer and organization of 16bit digital sound files with no loss of quality. Loss of quality was always the regrettable corollary of analogue transfers. Now, the fact that these machines can protect and retrieve information has interesting implications for the copyright and ownership, not to say the distribution of sound as a commodity. For example, equipment such as this is ideal for the storage and retrieval of digital sound files downloaded from the Internet. The day when we no longer buy records and CDs cannot be far away. – MH

Products

Matsushita Electric Industrial Co. Ltd
Portable MiniDisc Player – SJ-MJ7
recyclable magnesium alloy
h 1.7cm – w 7.2cm – l 8cm
h ⅝in – w 2⅞in – l 3⅛in
Matsushita Electric Industrial Co. – Japan

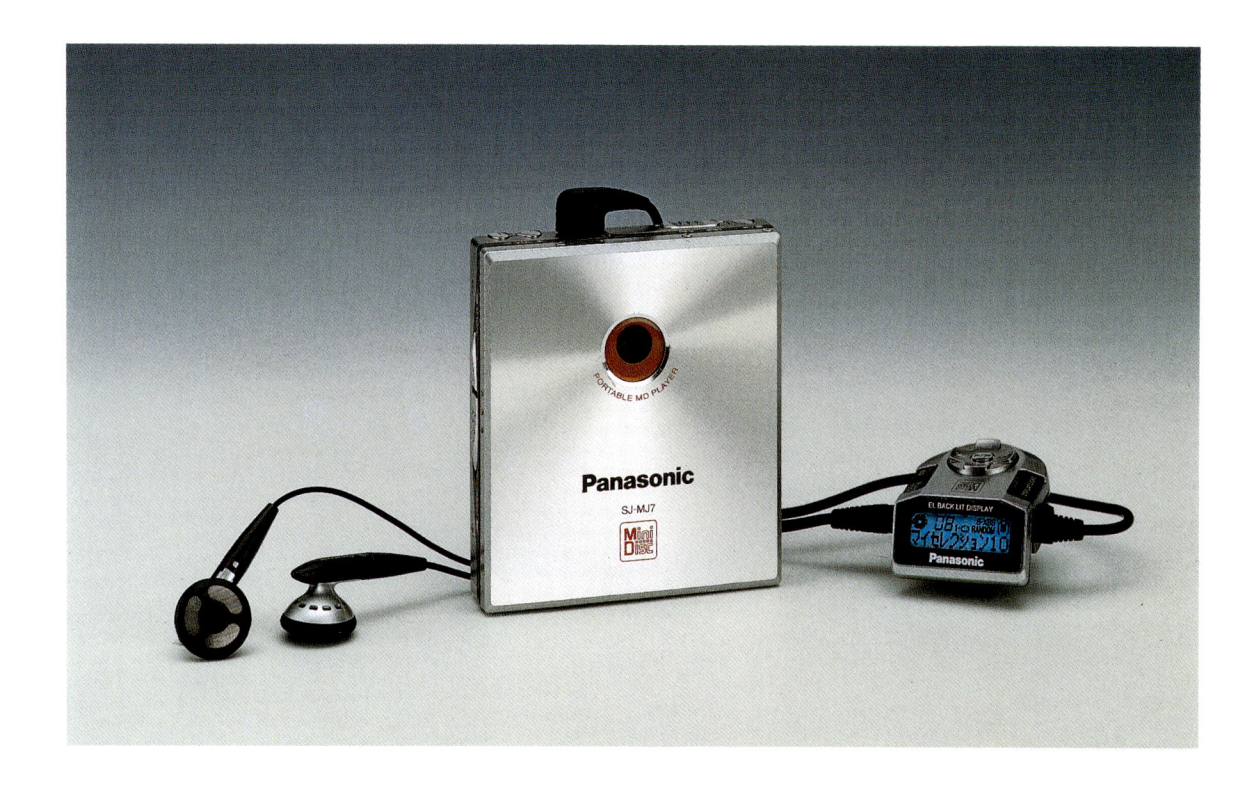

Yasuo Yuyama
MiniDisc Walkman – MZS-R5ST
aluminium – plastic
station – h 6.1cm – w 23.2cm – d 15.4cm
　　　　　h 2⅜in – w 9⅛in – d 6in
MD Walkman – h 2cm – w 11cm – d 7.7cm
　　　　　　　h ⅜in – w 4⅜in – d 3in
Sony Corp. – Japan

Mitsuhiro Nakamura and Takahiro Tsuge
Digital Recorder – NT-2
aluminium – ABS plastic
h 2.2cm – w 11.3cm – d 6.3cm
h ⅞in – w 4½in – d 2½in
Sony Corp. – Japan

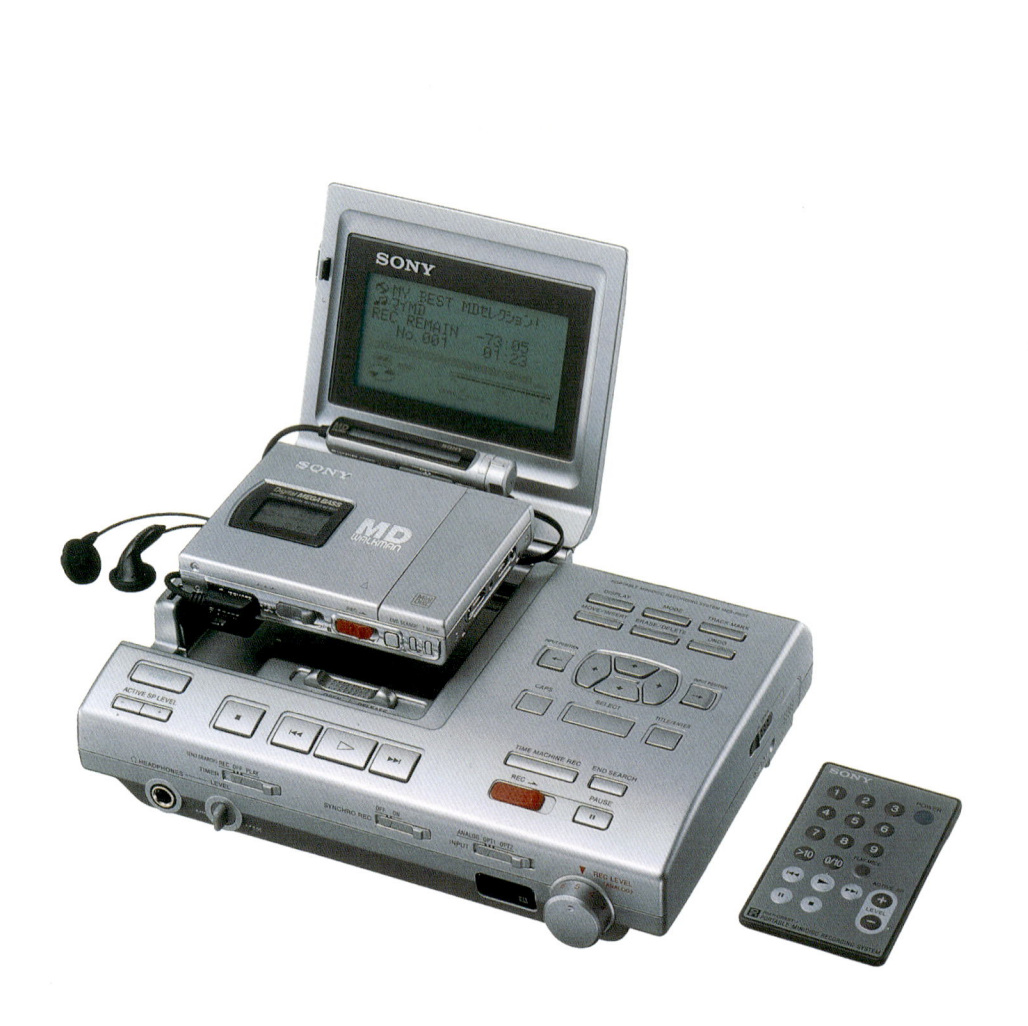

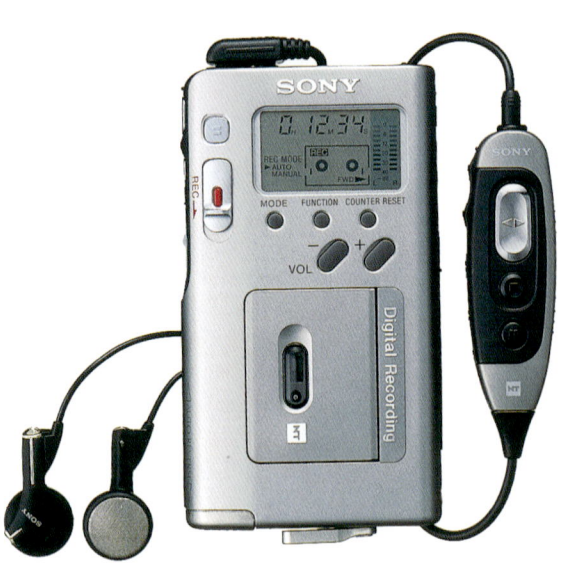

Products

Koji Shimobayashi
Digital Voice Recorder – D1000
aluminium – ABS
h 12cm – w 4.6cm
h 4¾in – w 1⅞in
Olympus Optical Co. – Japan

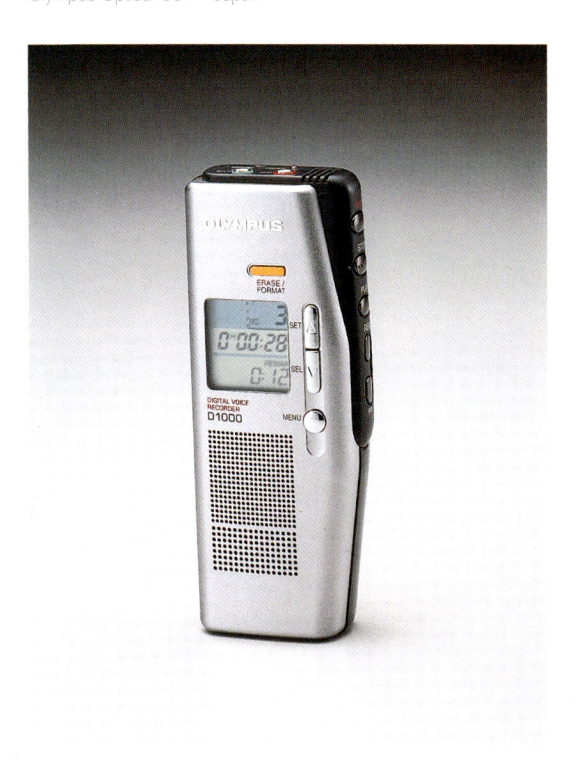

Yamaha Product Design Laboratory
Digital Mixing Console – Yamaha 01V
ABS – iron plate – glass
h 14.9cm – w 43cm – d 52cm
h 5⅞in – w 16⅞in – d 20½in
Yamaha Corporation – Japan

This array of equipment represents most of the applications that digital sound demands and creates. From music making to the creation of personal soundtracks, from digital note taking to the reorganization of your music library, the digital revolution demands the investment in new hardware by the humble consumer. This at least ought to be good news for the ailing Japanese and Pacific economies. – MH

Gerhard Heufler
Miniature Mine Detector – MIMID
carbon fibre
h 5.5cm – w 9.5cm – l 32.5cm/125cm
h 2⅛in – w 3¾in – l 12¾in/49¼in
Schiebel – Austria

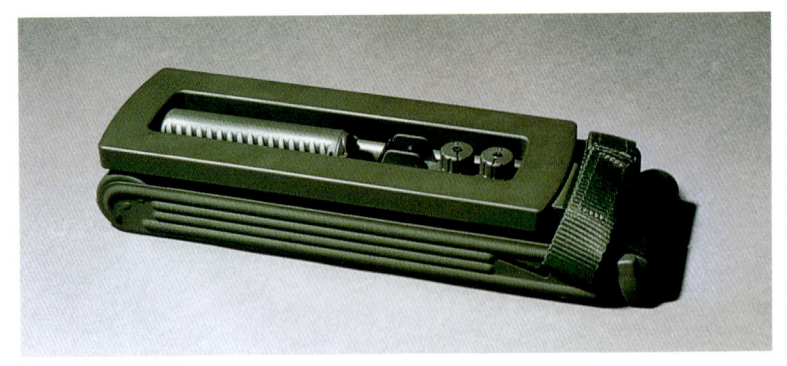

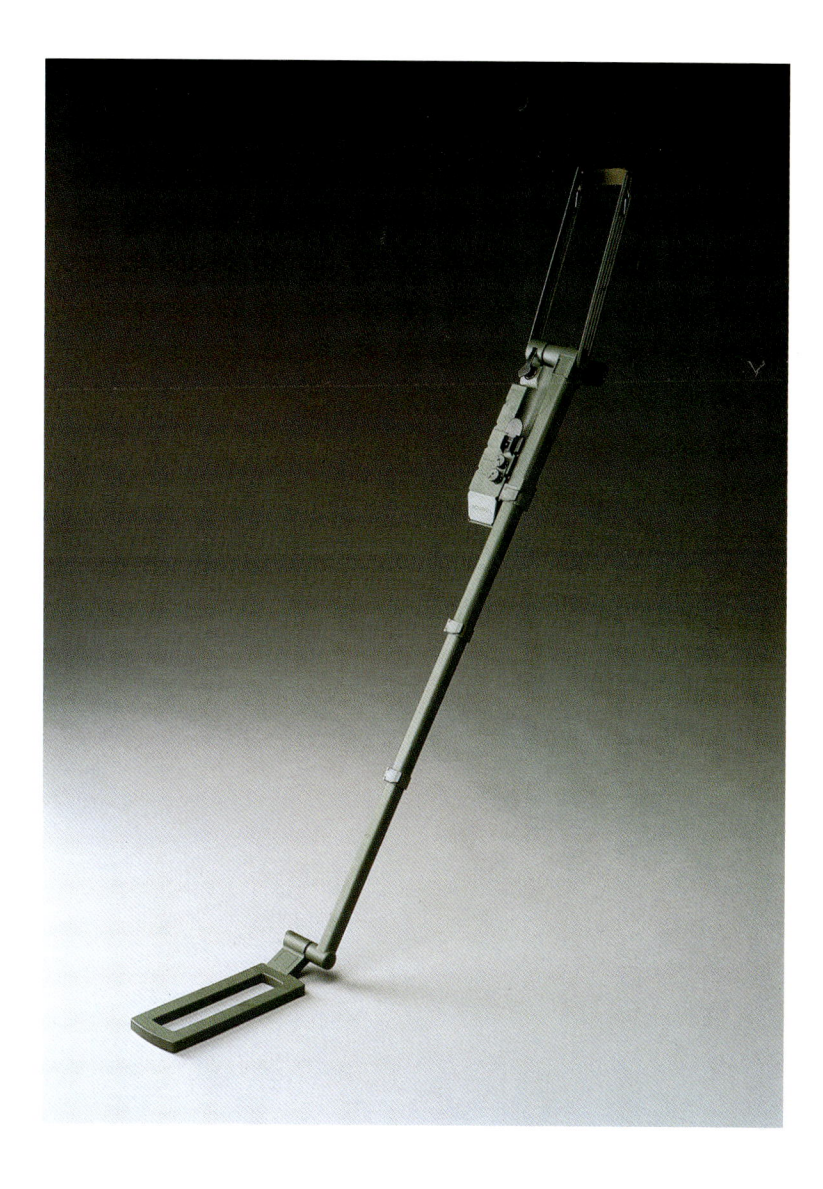

Products

Marc Newson
Watch – Hemipode Chronograph
h 1.6cm – di 4.4cm
h ⅝in – di 1¾in
Ikepod – Switzerland
limited edition

Products

Peter Gest
Toothbrush Rack
stainless steel
h 9cm – w 16cm – d 4cm
h 3½in – w 6¼in – d 1⅝in
Drop Design – Sweden

Defne Koz
Measuring Cup
stainless steel
h 13cm/17cm – di 8cm/11cm
h 5⅛in/6⅝in – di 3⅛in/4⅜in
WMF/21 – Germany

Products

De Padova srl
Candlestick – Copenhagen
silver-plate
h 13cm/26cm
h 5⅛in/10½in
De Padova – Italy

Yves Béhar
Trays – Lush Lily
cast aluminium
h 3cm – w 33cm – d 14cm
h 1⅛in – w 13in – d 5½in
Lush Lily – USA
limited batch production

These new takes on the humble tray recall the fascination with the tasks of the hostess/host which prevailed in the 1950s. The domestic accoutrements of the accomplished household have taken yet another turn here with the 'matching-tray-and-glasses' combination battling with the cool sculpture of the frozen ripple tray. Both pieces seem to imply domestic situations where conversation pieces are needed to break the ice. – MH

Products

Shinichi Sumikawa
Tray – Ripple
wood – Japanese lacquer
h 2cm – di 40cm
h ¾in – di 15¾in
Amano Shikki Co. – Japan

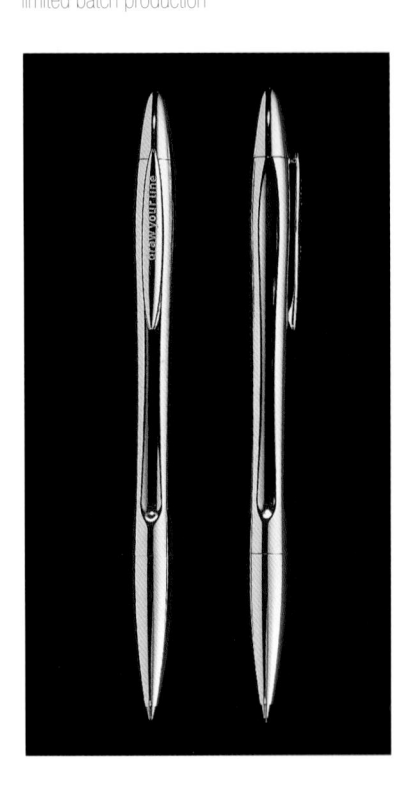

Adatte Design
Pen and Propelling Pencil – Draw Your Line
aluminium
l 14cm
l 5½in
limited batch production

Yamaha Product Design Laboratory
Wind Midi Controller – Yamaha WX5
plastics – ABS
h 7cm – w 6.2cm – l 61.1cm
h 2¾in – w 2½in – l 24in
Yamaha Corporation – Japan

Products

Olavi Lindén
Multipurpose Garden Cutter
aluminium — fibreglass-reinforced polyamide — steel
h 158cm — w 10cm — d 8cm
h 62¼in — w 3⅞in — d 3⅛in
Fiskars Consumer — Finland

Mark Sanders
Bicycle – Strida 2
aluminium – glass-reinforced polyamide
wheel – (base) 88.5cm – di 40.5cm
       (base) 34⁷⁄₈in – di 16in
seat height – max. 95cm – min. 75cm
             max. 37³⁄₈in – min. 29½in
Roland Plastics – UK

Products

Marco Ferreri
Shelving from the Barralibera System
anodized aluminium
h 123.5cm – w 73.5cm – d 23.5cm
h 48⅝in – w 28⅞in – d 9¼in
Agape – Italy

Giulio Cappellini and Roberto Palomba
Washbasin
ceramic
h 20cm – w 100cm – d 58cm
h 7⅞in – w 39⅜in – d 22⅞in
Ceramica Flaminia – Italy

Products

Ronan Bouroullec
Kitchen
polyurethane – polypropylene – aluminium
h 90cm – w 180cm/240cm – d 70cm
h 35⅜in – w 70⅞in/94½in – d 27½in
Units – Italy

The cool simplicity of these domestic interiors raises an interesting question. Namely: when does the configuration of furniture stop being interior design and become product design? The manufacture of whole rooms as a product is not new – *Domus* in the 1960s and 1970s regularly featured complete rooms which came as a monobloc which – like a Swiss Army pen knife – swung open and folded out and in upon themselves to answer every domestic need. Two of these designs are different in that they are assemblages of furniture and utilities to create a product. The third is a cupboard by any other name, albeit with a neat take on the problem of the door. – MH

Marc de Laat
Inflatable tent

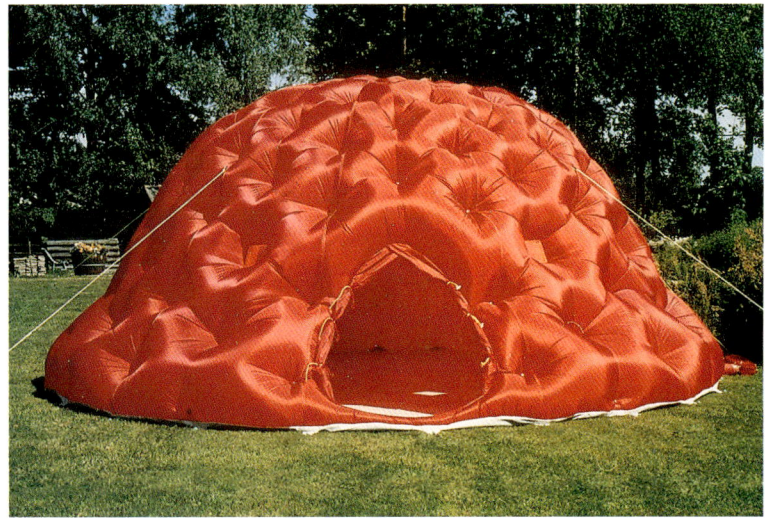

Products

Bisk Italia (Daf Griffith – Jonathan Ascough – Michael Macduff)
Box – Folio
SAN
h 5cm – w 35.5cm – d 7.5cm
h 2in – w 14in – d 3in
Ezech – Hong Kong

Karim Rashid
Holiday Bags – Tummy and Bow
extruded polypropylene sheet
h 10cm – w 43cm – l 29cm
h 4in – w 17in – l 11¼in
Issey Miyake – Japan

Products

CD Case
polyethylene
h 15cm – w 17cm – d 5cm
h 5⅞in – w 6⅝in – d 2in
Issey Miyake – Japan

Backpack – Spine
polypropylene – nylon
h 30cm – w 30cm – d 10cm
h 11⅞in – w 11⅞in – d 3⅞in
Issey Miyake – Japan

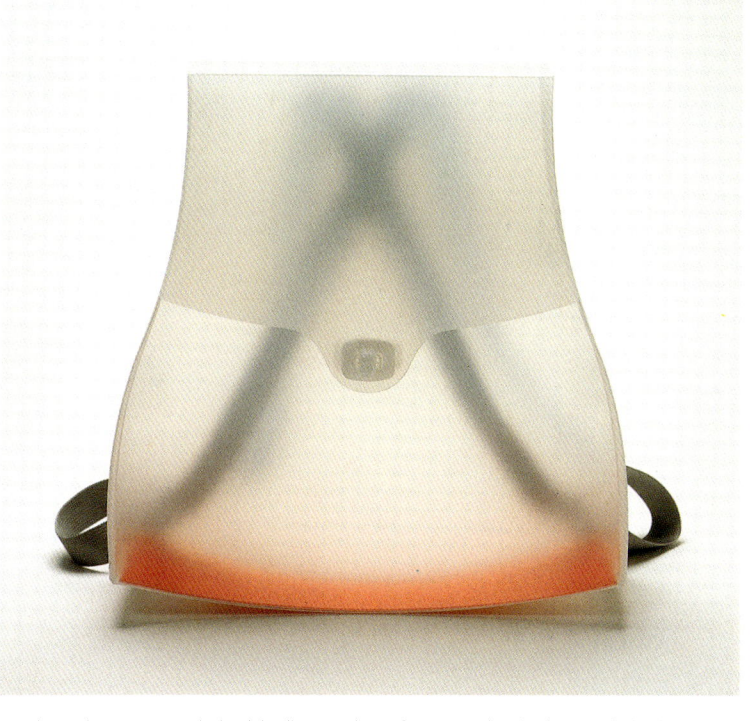

The translucent properties of extruded polypropylene and polyethylene have introduced a new and decidedly modern facet to the lexicon of design languages. Post tooling and development, production runs in these materials are very cheap and the results are malleable and readily available products of the petrochemical industries. Their flexibility and resilience means that for little money, products can be produced which depend as much on the inventiveness of the designer in developing new ways of cutting, folding and bending as they do on the vast industries which pull oil out of the ground and the ocean. – MH

Alfredo Häberli and Christophe Marchand
Fly Swatter
recyclable polypropylene
w 7cm – l 41.5cm – d 1cm
w 2¾in – l 16⅜in – d ⅜in
Authentics – Germany

Stefano Giovannoni
Box – Tutti-Frutti
PMMA – plastic
h 21cm – w 52cm – d 32cm
h 8¼in – w 20½in – d 12⅝in
Magis – Italy

Products

Coat Hanger – Bridge
PMMA – plastic
h 8cm – w 40cm – l 60cm
h 3 1/8in – w 15 3/4in – l 23 5/8in
Magis – Italy

Wristwatch – Volcano
plastic – silicone
h 2cm – w 4.5cm – l 25cm
h 3/4in – w 1 3/4in – l 9 7/8in
Seiko Corporation – Japan

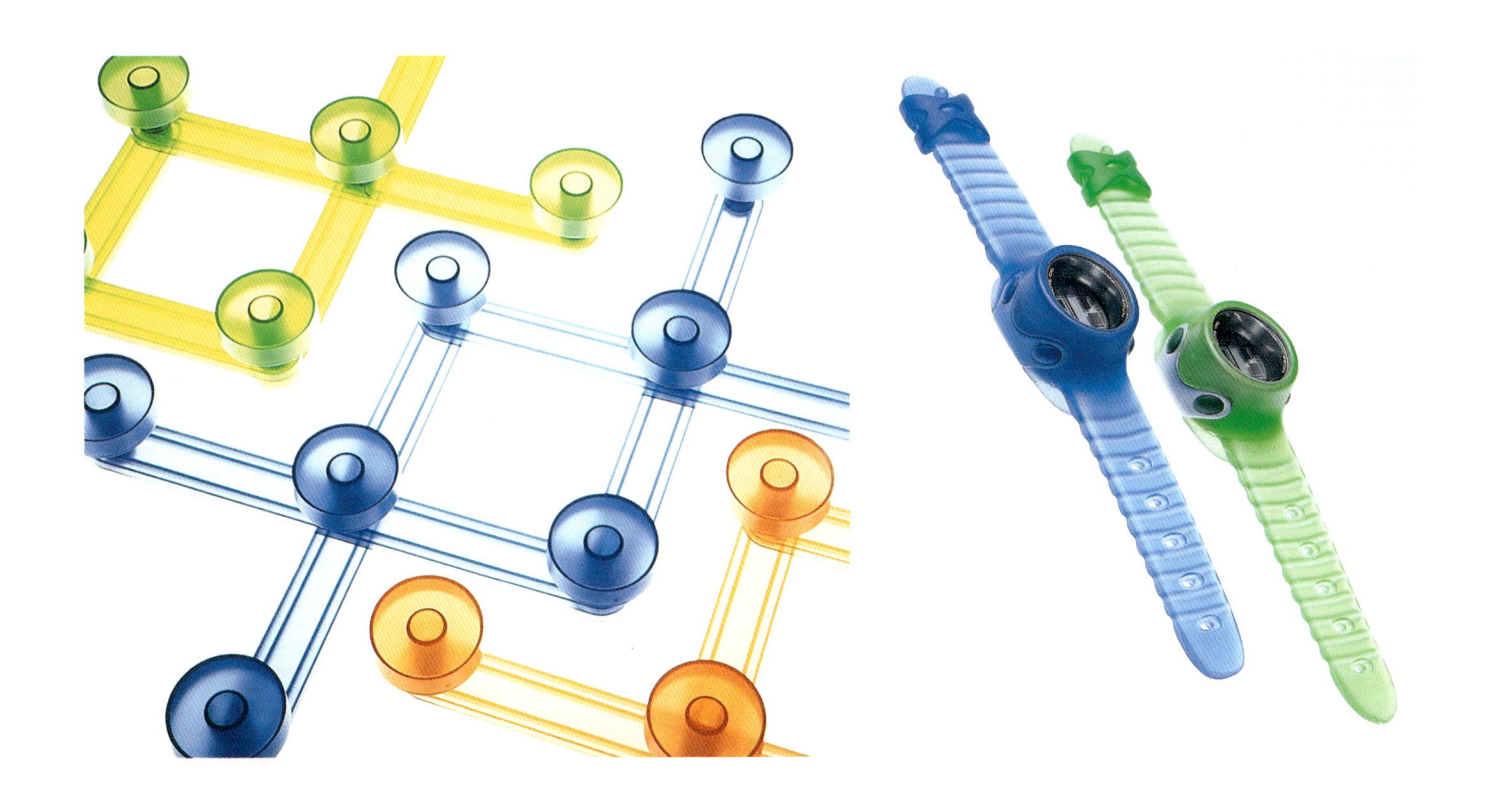

Marta Sansoni
Glass Mixer and Measure – Folpo
glass – thermoplastic resin
h 25.5cm – di 12.5cm
h 10in – di 5in
Alessi – Italy

Philippe Starck
Fly Swatter – Dr Skud
thermoplastic resin
h 44cm – w 9.3cm – d 6.7cm
h 17 3/8in – w 3 5/8in – d 2 5/8in
Alessi – Italy

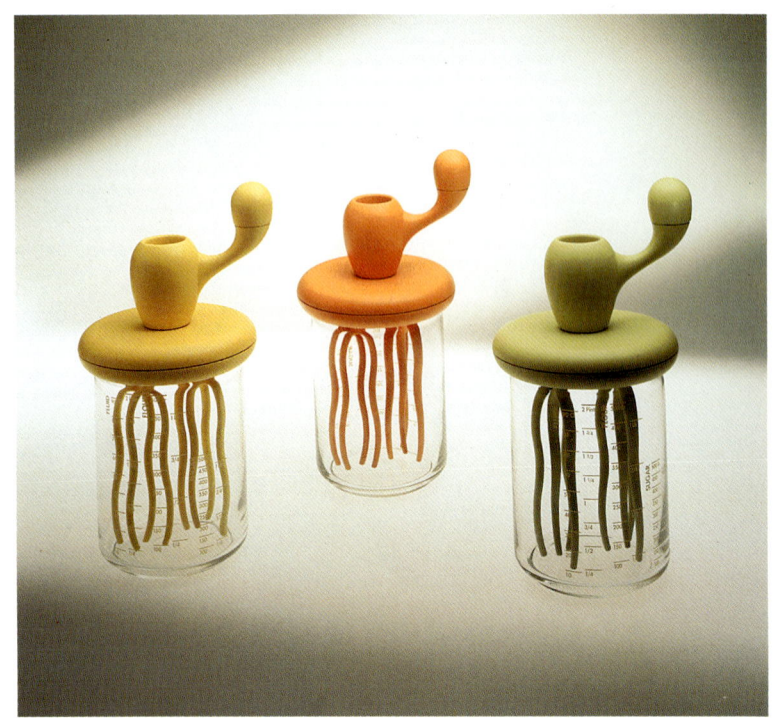

Products

Stefano Giovannoni
Broom – Mago
polypropylene
h 140cm – w 40cm – d 6.5cm
h 55⅛in – w 15¾in – d 2½in
Magis – Italy

Julian Brown
Adhesive Tape Dispenser – Hannibal
engineering polymer – metal
h 9.5cm – w 10.5cm – d 8cm
h 3¾in – w 4⅛in – d 3⅛in
Rexite – Italy

It had seemed for a while that the mighty Alessi corporation had the exclusive on the cutely rendered animal-as-domestic-goods product. It's interesting to see that there are designers who still wish to tap the semiotic potential of an object which looks as though it will deliver its stated function, in this case dispensing tape, whilst becoming your faithful little 'friend'. Part armadillo and part office staple, this machine is defying the stylistic Darwinism which ensures the extinction of animals/products that have characteristics extraneous to their survival. – MH

Enzo Mari
Colander – EM02
PP
h 14.5cm – di 20cm
h 5¾in – di 7⅞in
Alessi – Italy

Colander – EM03
PP
h 13.5cm – di 25cm
h 5⅜in – di 9⅞in
Alessi – Italy

Products

RADI Designers
Door Bell — Patrizia
silicone — polystyrene
d 6.7cm — di 9.5cm
d 2⅝in — di 3¾in
RADI Designers — France

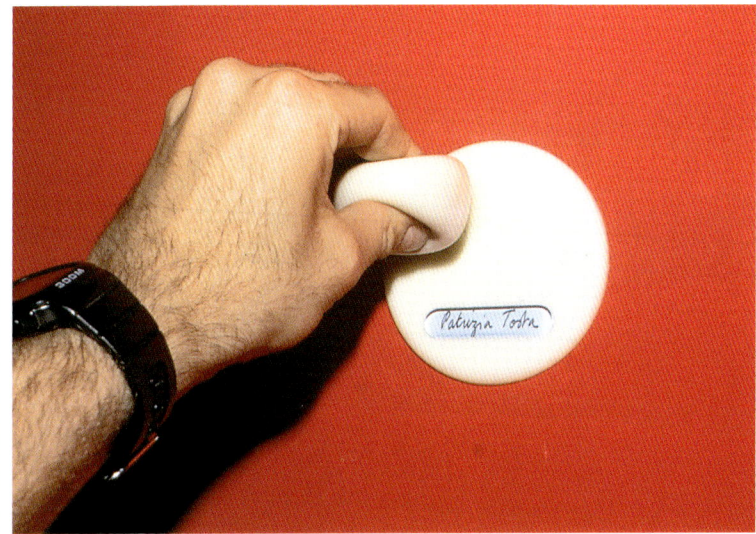

Ingrid Wiendels
Skirting Board – P103
rubber – aluminium
h 5.5cm – l unlimited – d 3.5cm
h 2⅛in – l unlimited – d 1⅜in
prototype

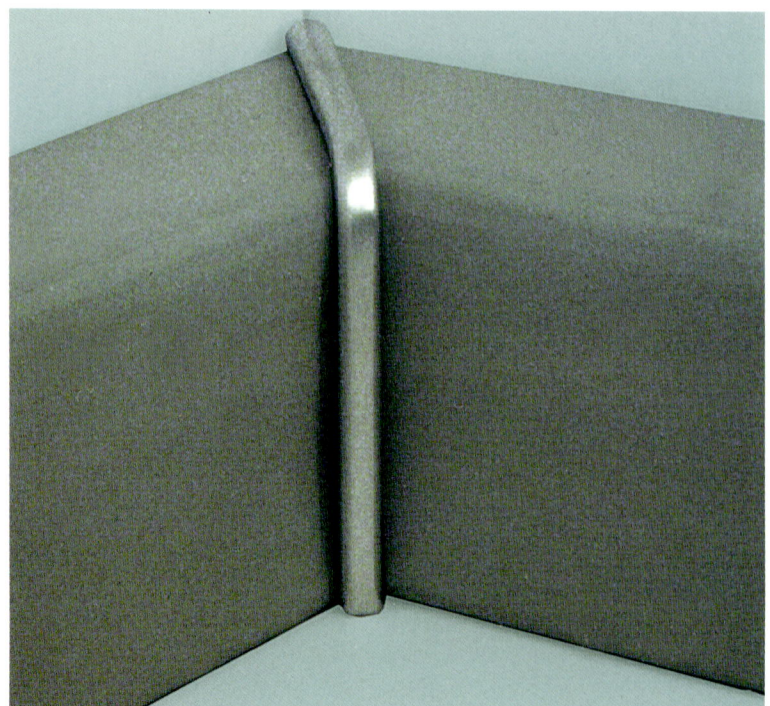

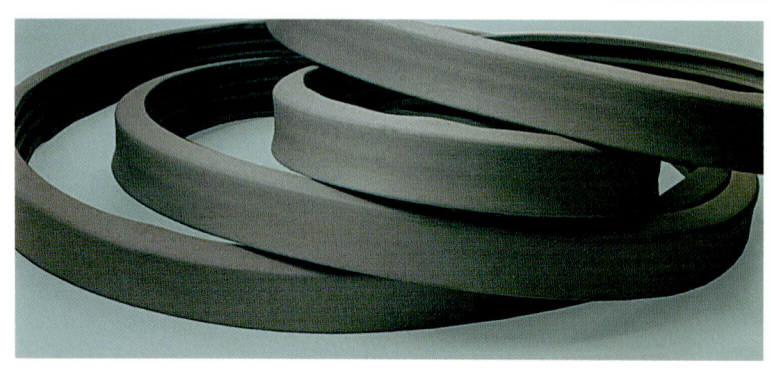

Products

Ingrid Wiendels
Skirting Board – P102
synthetics
h 5cm – l 500cm – d 1.5cm
h 2in – l 196⅞in – d ⅝in
prototype

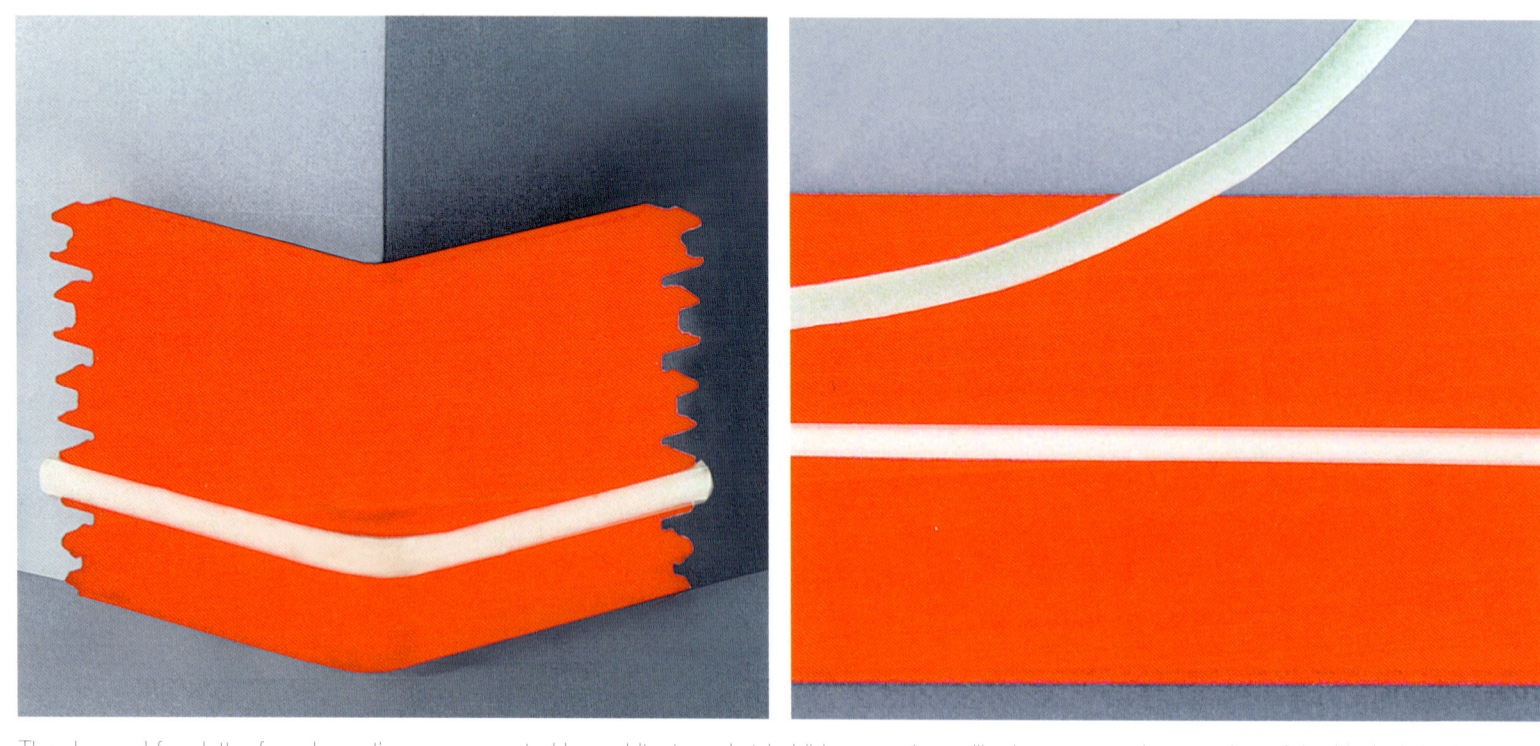

The demand for clutter-free domestic spaces created by architects and style bible magazines alike has spawned a mutation of the kind of ducting which is usually found in rooms that are homes to large amounts of electrical equipment. The duct has finally become a fashionable product. Furthermore, the change of use of many industrial premises to residential means that there are often floors which are solid concrete, or other load-bearing materials designed to support heavy goods and machinery. The use of the skirting board as duct means that wiring can be run through the biggest of spaces without having to disturb the flooring, whatever its make-up. – MH

Products

Biographies
Acquisitions
Photographic Credits
Suppliers

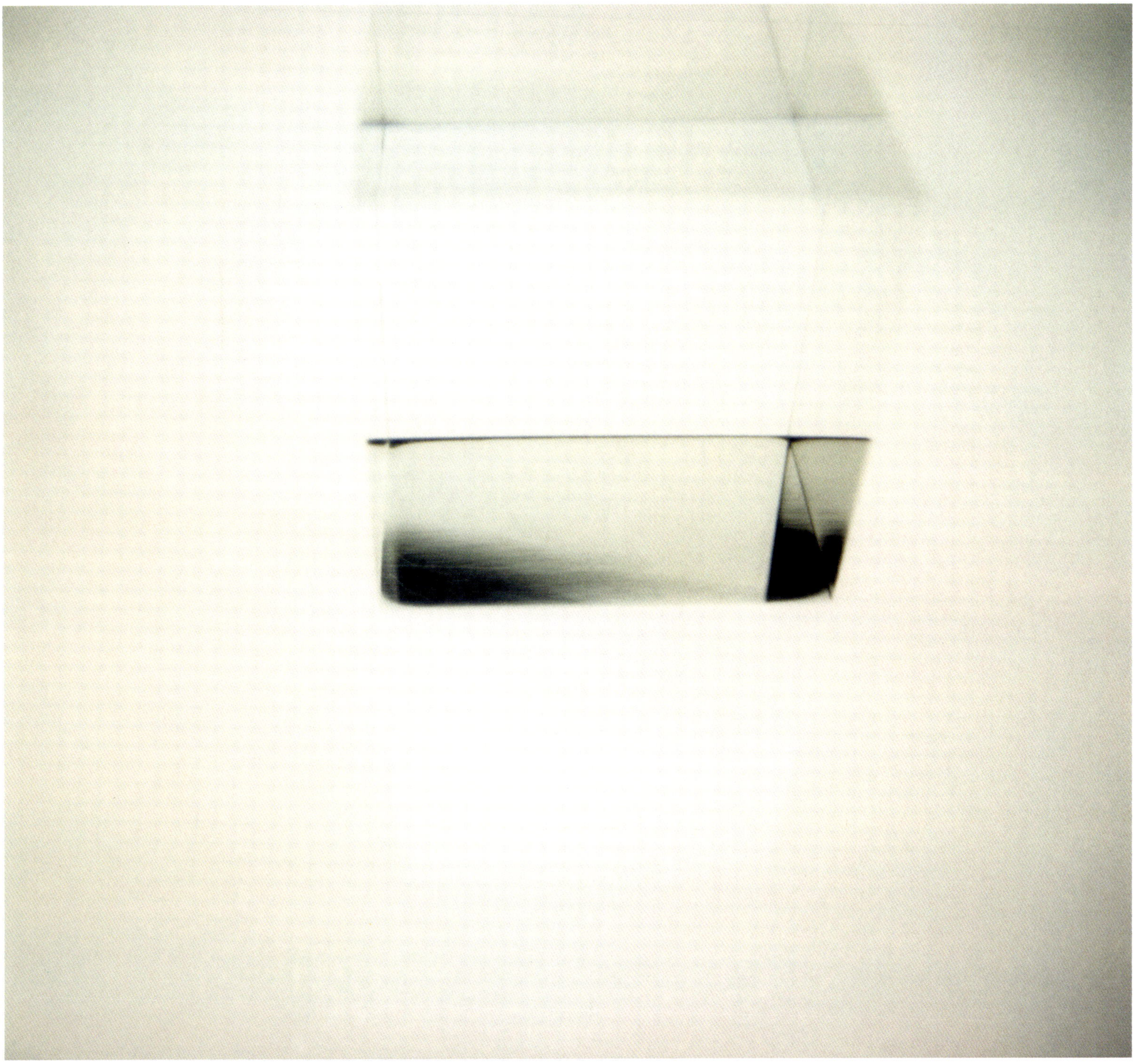

Adatte Design is a Swiss company founded in 1990 by Georges Adatte and Eric Giroud. The company is active in the fields of industrial design, packaging and graphic design. Clients include Belux, Philip Morris and Swissair. – 200

Ron Arad was born in Tel Aviv in 1951. He studied at the Jerusalem Academy of Art, and from 1974 to 1979 at the Architectural Association, London. In 1981 he founded One Off with Caroline Thorman. Well-known early pieces include the Rover Chair, the vacuum-packed Transformer Chair and the remote-controlled Aerial Light. Later work explored the use of tempered steel, first in the Well-Tempered Chair and later in the Bookworm. In 1988 Arad won the Tel Aviv Opera Foyer Interior Competition with C. Norton and S. McAdam, and the next year formed Ron Arad Associates with Caroline Thorman and Alison Brooks in order to realize the project, moving the firm's premises to Chalk Farm, London. Projects have included furniture design for Poltronova, Vitra, Moroso and Driade; the design of various interior installations; the interiors of the restaurants Belgo and Belgo Centraal in London, domestic architectural projects and the winning competition entry for the Adidas Stadium, Paris (unbuilt). Arad was a guest professor at the Hochschule in Vienna from 1994 to 1997 and is currently Professor of Furniture Design at the Royal College of Art in London. – 58

Les Ateliers du Nord was founded by Antoine Cahen and Claude Frossard. Cahen graduated in industrial design from Lausanne Art School, where he later taught from 1980 to 1985. He opened his own studio in 1984 and started his partnership with Frossard a few years later. Frossard served an apprenticeship as a draughtsman before entering the industrial design department of Lausanne Art School. He worked for the Swiss Foreign Affairs Department at the Pakistan Design Institute in Karachi before co-founding Les Ateliers du Nord. The practice is concerned with product and equipment design. In 1998 the practice was awarded an IF Distinction in Hanover for the Leclanche SL Light and for the Espresso System C220 coffee machine. – 102

Shin and Tomoko Azumi studied industrial design at Kyoto City University of Art and the Royal College of Art, London. In 1996 they were finalists in the Blueprint/100% Design Awards. They founded Azumi's in 1995, undertaking projects for British, Italian and Japanese clients. They have exhibited at Sotheby's and at the Crafts Council, London. – 62

Emmanuel Babled was born in France in 1967, and today lives and works in both Milan and Venice. He studied at the Istituto Europeo di Disegno in Milan, then worked for several years with Prospero Rasulo and Gianni Veneziano at Studio Oxido in Milan. He has been working as a freelance designer since the early 1990s for clients such as Fine Factory, Steel, Casprini, Wedgwood, Waterford Crystal Ltd, Kundalini and Rosenthal. Since 1995 he has also been an independent producer of Murano glass vases and ceramic items for IDEE Co. Ltd, Tokyo. – 124

Gijs Bakker was born in Amersfoort, The Netherlands, in 1942. He studied at the Instituut voor Kunstnijverheidsonderwijs, Amsterdam and the Konstfackskolan in Stockholm where he graduated in industrial design. He founded a jewellery workshop with his wife in 1966, whilst at the same time working as a freelance designer involved with interior, exhibition and product design. He has taught at various design institutions in The Netherlands and in 1987 was appointed professor at the Design Academy in Eindhoven. He co-founded Droog Design with Remy Ramakers in 1993, and Chi ha Paura Contemporary Jewellery with Marijke Vallanzasca three years later. Since 1997 he has collaborated with Rosenthal who have manufactured Droog Design porcelain items. – 129

Philip Baldwin see **Monica Guggisburg**

Enrico Baleri was born in Albino, Italy in 1942. He studied architecture at Milan Polytechnic. While still a student he was invited by Dino Gavina to open a furnishing centre in Bergamo. In 1968 he founded a research group in Milan and has since designed collections and furniture for Gavina, Flos, Knoll International and Alias, a firm he set up in 1979. He was art director for Alias until 1983. In 1984 he and his wife Marilisa Baleri Decimo started Baleri Italia, collaborating with Hollein, Mendini and other designers such as Starck, Dalisi and Wettstein. Since 1986 Baleri has been active in the fields of architecture, image and communication, promotional graphics and industrial design. – 32

Miguel Vieira Baptista was born in 1968 and lives in Lisbon. As a post-graduate he studied product design at the Glasgow School of Art, and he is currently working in the fields of industrial design and exhibitions with companies such as Proto Design, Bastidor and Centro Cultural de Belem. – 84

Barber Osgerby Associates was founded in 1996 by Edward Barber and Jay Osgerby who met when they were studying together at the Royal College of Art, London. The practice has designed interiors for residential and commercial premises and has had furniture manufactured by Cappellini and the Conran shops. Their latest project is the Soho Brewing Company – a microbrewery and restaurant in London. They were awarded Best New Designers in 1998 at the International Contemporary Furniture Fair in New York. Recent projects include a pharmacy and herbal apothecary interior and a flagship hair salon for Trevor Sorbie. – 63

Roberto Barbieri was born in Milan in 1942 and studied architecture at Milan Polytechnic. He has collaborated with Zanotta since 1994. – 20

François Bauchet was born in 1948 and today practises interior and furniture design in Saint Etienne, France. His interior design projects include the reception areas of the Musée d'Art et d'Industrie, Saint Etienne and the Centre d'Art de Vassiviere in Limousin. He has exhibited his work in Europe and Japan and has had several one-man shows at Galerie Néotù, Paris. His work can be seen in the permanent collection of the Musée des Arts Décoratifs in Paris. – 17

Yves Béhar was born in Switzerland in 1967, and graduated from the Art Center College of Design in 1991. He is the founding principal of VOID (Virtual Office of Integrated Design), an international product design consultancy based in San Francisco. As design manager for frogdesign and previously for Lunar Design, he is widely noted for designing brand products such as the Silicon Graphics workstation and Hewlett Packard Pavilion line of personal computers. International design prizes have been awarded to Béhar by 5 IDEA, Annual Design Review, SMAU (Italy), and IF Industrie Hanover. Béhar is a professor of design at CCAC. – 198

Mario Bellini was born in 1935 and graduated in architecture from Milan Polytechnic in 1959. He began to design products and furniture in 1963 and has collaborated with numerous Italian and international manufacturers. Completed architectural projects include the office building of the AEM Thermoelectric Power Plant at Cassano d'Abba; the Milan Trade Fair Extension; the Tokyo Design Centre; the Schmidtbank Headquarters in Germany; the Arsoa Company Headquarters in Yamanashi-ken and the Natuzzi Americas Inc. Headquarters in North Carolina. He is currently undertaking projects in both Russia and Dubai. He has lectured at leading design schools throughout the world and since 1995 has taught in the School of Architecture at the University of Genoa. He was the editor of *Domus* from 1986 to 1991. Bellini has received many awards for his professional work including seven Compasso d'Oro prizes. – 46

Sebastian Bergne studied at the Royal College of Art, London and worked in Hong Kong and Milan before forming his own practice in 1990. Clients include Cassina, Vitra, Oluce, Authentics and Driade. He is a visiting tutor at Central Saint Martin's College of Art and Design and the London Institute, and was a jury member for the Design Week Awards in 1991. He has taken part in group shows in London, New York, Hamburg, Tokyo and Brussels, most recently 'Mutant Materials in Contemporary Design' at the Museum of Modern Art, New York in 1995 and in 1997 a one-man show at the International Contemporary Furniture Fair in New York. – 80, 84

Carlo Bimbi received his degree from the ISIA, Florence and worked with various Italian furniture designers before founding Internotredici Associati with Gianni Ferrara and Nilo Gioacchini. He now has his own studio in Florence. From 1970 to 1990 he was professor of design at the Istituto d'Arte, Florence and from 1982 to 1983 he taught at the ISIA. He has collaborated with many leading manufacturers including B&B, I Guzzini and Segis and has participated in numerous competitions, conventions and exhibitions internationally. – 50

Bisk Italia is a Milan-based design studio founded in 1990 by Daf Griffith, Jonathan Ascough and Michael Macduff who all attended Brighton University, England. The company is active in the fields of architectural model making and product design and collaborates with design studios such as De Lucchi, Sottsass Associati and Renzo Piano. – 208

Matz Borgström was born in Stockholm in 1954. He trained in the interior and industrial design departments of the Konstfack in Stockholm. He has collaborated with companies such as IKEA, Orrefors and Asplund and is also head teacher at the Beckmans School of Design and senior master at the Konstfack. He has received many national awards and has won scholarships to study in Paris and the USA. – 148

Ronan Bouroullec was born in Quimper (Bretagne), France, in 1971. He graduated in applied and decorative art and has worked on a freelance basis since 1995. His furniture designs have been produced by Cappellini, Units, Christian Liaigre and Domeau et Peres and his objects by Cappellini, Ex Novo, Ligne Roset, Ardi, Galerie Néotù and La Monnaie de Paris. He has held group and solo exhibitions in France, most recently at the 'Made in France' show at the Centre Georges Pompidou, Paris. – 114–17, 125, 126, 127, 158, 205

Constantin Boym was born in Moscow in 1955. He graduated from the Moscow Architectural Institute in 1978 and from 1984 to 1985 studied for a Masters degree in design at the Domus Academy in Milan. He became a registered architect in the USA in 1988 and today has his own design consultancy in New York. He has designed award-winning products for many international companies including Morphos, Néotù and the Formica Corporation. Since 1986 he has taught at the Parsons School of Design, New York, where he currently serves as the director of product studies in the department of product design. Awards include the ID Annual Design Award (1988 and 1990). His work is included in the permanent collections of the Cooper-Hewitt National Design Museum, New York and the Musée des Arts Décoratifs in Montreal. – 112

Laurene Leon Boym was born in 1964 in New Jersey. She obtained a BFA from the School of Visual Arts in 1986 and an MID from the Pratt Institute in 1993. A founder member of the Association of Women Industrial Designers, she co-curated 'Goddess in the Details: Product Design by Women in 1990'. In 1993 she was appointed Designer in Residence at the Cooper-Hewitt National Design Museum and since 1994 has been junior-year studio teacher in the product design department at the Parsons School of Design. She has exhibited her work widely throughout the United States and took part in the landmark exhibition 'Mechanical Bridges' at the Cooper-Hewitt in the early 1990s. – 112

Andrea Branzi was born in 1938 in Florence. He studied architecture, then founded the avant-garde group Archizoom Associates together with Gilberto Corretti, Paolo Deganello and Massimo Morozzi in 1966. From 1974 to 1976 he was involved with Global Tools, and in the late 1970s set up CDM, a Milan-based group of design consultants. He worked with Studio Alchimia and Memphis from the outset, designing furniture and objects and preparing shows and publications. He founded the Domus Academy in 1983 and has been its cultural director and vice-president. He also teaches and holds conferences at universities in Italy and abroad. He has held many one-man shows at the Milan Triennale and at galleries and museums around the world. All his projects were acquired in 1982 by the Communications Study Centre and Archives at the University of Parma. In 1987 Branzi won the Compasso d'Oro prize in recognition of his whole career. – 95

Barbara Brenner was born in Stuttgart in 1939. She worked for Rosenthal AG from 1960 to 1968 and for Studio Tapia Wirkkala Design in Helsinki. Since 1968 she has worked as a freelance textile designer, ceramicist and book illustrator, and since 1984 has taught textile design at the Fachschule in Hanover. – 168

Fernando Brízio was born in 1968 and lives in Lisbon. He graduated in product design from the Escola Superior de Belas Artes in Lisbon. He worked for Proto Design before moving to the Filipe Alarcao studio. – 85

Julian Brown was born in Northampton, UK, in 1955. He graduated from the Royal College of Art in London and completed his training by working for a design studio in Austria. He has since designed for many international companies and has a long-standing connection with the Hochschule der Künste in Berlin where he was a guest professor in 1992. – 213

Debbie Jane Buchan was born in 1973. She has an MA in Art and Design and a BA in Surface Decoration. In 1995 she was selected for the New Designers Exhibition in London and has also shown her work in Scotland and Japan. – 146

Stephen Burks was born in 1969 and studied architecture at the Illinois Institute of Technology and product design at ITT's Institute of Design. He also attended Columbia University's Graduate School of Architecture. Before launching Readymade, he worked as a designer at Prescriptives, Siegel & Gale, IDEE Co. (Tokyo), Fitch Inc. (Boston), the Arnell Group and Swatch Creative Lab, Milan. He has hosted a design workshop at the Ecole des Beaux Arts de Saint-Etienne in France, and lectured at the Beckmans School of Design seminar, Stockholm, in 1998. – 66

Christof Burtscher and Patrizia Bertolini studied carpentry and sculpture, and fine art and industrial design respectively. They have worked together since 1991 and have received a number of international awards and prizes, most recently Young & Design 1997 in Milan. – 68

Antoine Cahen see **Les Ateliers du Nord**

Biographies

Fernando and Humberto Campana have worked together since 1984. Humberto trained as a lawyer and Fernando, his brother, graduated as an architect. Their work involves research into combining different materials. They have held many individual shows in Brazil and have taken part in group exhibitions in Brazil, Italy and the USA, most recently in the 'O Brazil Faz Design' show at the Milan Furniture Fair, 1998. They have been honoured in their own country, receiving the Primeiro Premio and Segundo Categorias Moveis Resdidencias in 1997 and 1998 respectively. – 75

Achille Castiglioni, born in Milan in 1918, began his career after the Second World War with his brothers Livio and Pier Giacomo. He is well known for his innovative designs in interiors, furniture and lighting and his clients include Flos, Phonola, Bernini, Cassina, de Padova, Fontana Arte, Interflex, Kartell, Marcatré, Olivetti, Up and Up and Zanotta. Castiglioni is one of the foremost talents in Italian design and has been honoured nine times with the Compasso d'Oro. He was one of the founder members of the Industrial Design Association (ADI). In 1985 he became an honorary member of the Committee of Advisors at the Art Center College of Design in Pasadena, California and in Montreaux, Switzerland. In 1986 he was made an honorary member of the Faculty of Royal Designers for Industry at the Royal Society of Art in London and twelve months later he obtained the 'Honoris Causa' degree at the Royal College of Art in London. His work is in the collections of the Victoria and Albert Museum, London; the Museum of Modern Art, New York; the Israel Museum, Jerusalem and in museums in Prague, Zurich, Munich, Düsseldorf, Cologne, Hamburg and Helsinki. He was professor of industrial design and decoration at the University of Milan from 1969 to 1993. – 63, 78

Antonio Citterio was born in Meda, Italy, in 1950 and has been involved in industrial and furniture design since 1967. He studied at Milan Polytechnic and in 1973 set up a studio with Paolo Nava. The two have worked jointly and individually for B & B Italia and Flexform, among other clients. In 1979 they were awarded the Compasso d'Oro. In 1987 Terry Dwan became a partner in Studio Citterio Dwan, and the company has undertaken many interior design projects since then, including a range of schemes for Esprit and offices and showrooms for Vitra. Among the work realized in Japan, in partnership with Toshiyuki Kita, is the headquarters in Kobe for World Company, the Corente Building in Tokyo, and, in 1992, the Daigo headquarters in Tokyo. Citterio has taught at the Domus Academy in Milan and has participated in many exhibitions including independent shows in Hanover, Rome, Amsterdam, Paris and Weil am Rhein. In 1993 he designed the layout of the exhibition 'Antonio Citterio and Terry Dwan' promoted by Arc en Rêve in Bordeaux, which travelled to Osaka and Tokyo in 1994. In 1996 Antonio Citterio and Partners participated in numerous design competitions including the corporate design for the Commerzbank pilot branches in Germany, the new retail environment for Habitat in Paris and the restructuring of the existing Line 1 metro system of Milan (all under construction). – 21, 25, 36, 139

Claesson Koivisto Rune was formed by Mårten Claesson, Eero Koivisto and Ola Rune who met at the Konstfack University College of Arts, Crafts and Design in Stockholm. Prior to this Claesson and Koivisto had studied at the Parsons School of Design in New York in the department of architecture and environmental design, and Rune in the interior and furniture design department of the Royal Academy of Art in Copenhagen. Since beginning their collaboration they have received numerous prizes including the Guldstolen (Golden Chair) Honorary Award by the Swedish Society of Interior Architects for the best interior design project, and the Grand Prix Formex – best overall exhibition design at the Formex Design Fair in 1998. All three partners teach at various institutions in Sweden and Ola Rune was head teacher at the Beckmans School of Design in Stockholm from 1997 to 1998. Claesson, Koivisto and Rune participated in over 50 object and furniture design exhibitions in Sweden and abroad between 1990 and 1997. – 35, 144

Comma was founded by David Khouri and Roberto Guzman who presented their first furniture collection at the International Contemporary Furniture Fair in New York in 1998. Khouri is originally from California and moved to New York to attend Columbia University graduate school where he received a Master of Architecture and a Master of Science in Historic Preservation. Prior to co-founding his practice he worked for Bohn Associates, designing retail and showroom projects. Guzman also attended Columbia, graduating with a Masters in Architecture in 1987. He has worked for various architects including Kohn Pedersen Fox and Peter Marino Association. He has also worked in set design and as an assistant art director for the 1996 Summer Olympics and the 1997 Grammy Awards. He is currently working on a residence in London. – 52

Björn Dahlström was born in Stockholm in 1957. He has designed furniture for cbi and technically advanced designs such as the Cobra beaker for Atlas Copco. His work is exhibited in various design collections including the Victoria and Albert Museum in London. – 29, 134–7

Paul Daly was born in Dublin in 1963. He trained at the National College of Art in Dublin and at Goldsmiths College, London, then moved to New York and worked with artists and sculptors as well as with the design group Clodagh and architect Robert Pierpont. He returned to London in 1989 and set up his own design and sculpture studio. From 1991 Daly developed his interest in interior design, creating the Interim Art Gallery in London; the Ri-Ra club; the Ted Baker Shop; the Elbow Room bar and Ozwald Boateng's fashion showroom in Savile Row. Since 1997 Daly has been working on restaurants in London, Newcastle and Leeds. He continues to produce new furniture lines and also collaborates with the band U2, most recently on their 97/98 'Pop Mart' tour. – 65

Giovanni D'Ambrosio was born in 1959. He studied architecture and advertising graphics in Rome, then worked for 10 years in various architectural studios. Since 1995 he has been a member of the Industrial Design Association (ADI) and is also a member of Consiglio Superiore dell'Istituto Nazionale di Architettura. He won the award for the best stand at the National Association of Tourism and was nominated at the national contest, INARCH in 1992 for the Nordica stand in Munich. – 99

Marc de Laat graduated from the Design Academy, Eindhoven in 1996. In 1998 he started his own studio specializing in interior design and domestic product design. – 206

Michele de Lucchi was born in Ferrara, Italy, in 1951 and graduated from Florence University in 1975. During his student years he founded the Gruppo Cavart, a group concerned with avant-garde and conceptual architecture. He designed for Alchimia until the establishment of Memphis in 1981. He was responsible for the design of the Memphis exhibitions and his most important works included a series of new household appliances and the prefabricated holiday houses that were shown at the Milan Triennali in 1979 and 1983. Today he produces art-orientated handmade products, industrial consumer items and furniture. In 1986 he founded and promoted Solid, a group of young designers developing new design concepts, and in 1990 Produzione Privata, a production company for experimental objects. He is a consultant for Olivetti, responsible for the design of all the company's products, banking machines and office furniture systems. His architectural activities range from shop design to large-scale office buildings and private apartment blocks. De Lucchi has taught at design schools and universities such as the Domus Academy, Milan and the University of Detroit. He holds seminars on design management for the MBA course at the Università Commerciale Luigi Bocconi in Milan. – 81, 82

Christian Deuber is one of the founder members of the N2 group in Lucerne, Switzerland. While training as an electrical engineer, he gained experience in lighting design and set up his own studio, Pharus Lighting Design. – 95

Tom Dixon was born in Sfax, Tunisia, in 1959 and moved to the UK when he was four years old. He formed Creative Salvage with Nick Jones and Mark Brazier-Jones in 1985. His studio, Space, is where his prototypes and commissioned works – stage sets, furniture, sculpture, illuminated sculpture, architectural installations, chandeliers and other objects – are made. His clients include Cappellini, Comme des Garçons, Nigel Coates, Ralph Lauren, Vivienne Westwood and Terence Conran. Dixon has exhibited work internationally, most recently in 'A New Century in Design' at the National Museum of Modern Art, Tokyo. His designs are in the permanent collections of the Victoria and Albert Museum, London; the Musée des Arts Décoratifs and the Centre Georges Pompidou, Paris; the Vitra Chair Museum, Basle; the Crafts Council and the Design Museum, London; and the Brooklyn Museum, New York. In 1994 Dixon opened the Space shop. He is currently head of design at Habitat UK. – 26, 157

Bruno Fattorini is the president of the Italian manufacturer MDF and is also its lead designer and art director. Throughout the 1990s he has been involved in the development of a collection of bookcases, partitions, tables, beds and accessories that includes wardrobes as well as kitchen units. His Minima shelving system was awarded the 1998 ADI Compasso d'Oro Honorary Mention. – 73

Roberto Feo graduated from the Royal College of Art, London, in 1997 and, with Rosario Hurtado and Francisco Santos, created 'el ultimo grito', a design and product development company specializing in furniture, lighting and interiors. – 75

Marco Ferreri was born in Imperia, Italy, in 1958 and graduated from Milan Polytechnic in 1981. He opened his own office in 1984 and is active in the fields of industrial design, architecture, graphics, art direction and set design. His work can be found in the collections of the Museum of Modern Art, New York and the Israel Museum, Jerusalem. His Libroletto collection for Bruno Munari and Less chair by Nemo were both selected for the 40th Compasso d'Oro Competition. He was responsible for the 'Segnalibro' and 'Matite' exhibitions, which toured Italy and Europe, as well as the exhibition 'Face, Italian Designer Gallery' at the International Contemporary Furniture Fair, New York which he arranged in collaboration with *Abitare* magazine. – 204

Uwe Fischer founded Ginbande with Klaus Achim Heine in 1985. They both studied at the Hochschule für Gestaltung, Offenbach, specializing in industrial design and visual communication respectively. Ginbande works on corporate identities for public and private companies, and its experimental two- and three-dimensional pieces are regularly exhibited. – 45

Michal Fronek and Jan Nemecek were born in 1966 and 1963 respectively. Both studied at the Academy of Applied Arts in Prague under Borek Sipek. They began their first collaboration as the design group Olgoj Chorchoj shortly after attending a summer workshop at the Vitra Design Museum, and have completed numerous interior design projects in Prague. Artel II was founded in 1993 and exhibited at the Milan Furniture Fair; the International Conference of Arts and Crafts, London; the International Design Exhibition, Turin; and the Gallery Genia Loci, Prague. Fronek and Nemecek have taught alongside Sipek at the Academy of Applied Arts in Prague and were responsible for designing the interior fittings in Vaclav Havel's Prague house. Recent commissions include the design of a fire staircase at the Academy of Fine Arts; the design of a jeans shop and sports shop in Bratislava; and the reconstruction and interior design of a penthouse for *Elle* magazine (all 1996). In 1997 they received an Honorable Award, Grand Prix of the Czech Association of Architects. – 70

Naoto Fukasawa was born in Kofu, Japan, in 1956 and graduated in industrial design from the Tama Art University. He was chief designer at R&D design group and Seiko Epson Corporation before joining IDEO San Francisco. Still with IDEO, he returned to Japan in 1996 and is now head of their branch in Tokyo. He has won three major design awards for a patient-support device for Baxter Healthcare and for his stacking chair for Metro Furniture. His work is in the permanent collection of the San Francisco Museum of Modern Art, and he has lectured at the California College of Arts and Crafts, Stanford University, the Royal College of Art, London and Tama Art University. – 175, 176, 180

Rock Galpin was born in London in 1966. He graduated from Central Saint Martin's College of Art and Design with an MA in industrial design. In 1995 he set up Studio Orange, designing furniture and products aimed at serial production. These products have been exhibited in Cologne, Hanover, Milan, New York and in the UK. Commissions have included sofas and tables for Aram Designs; household products for Authentics and television and furniture designs for sets. Galpin designed his own converted warehouse studio in Shoreditch, London, which has received international press attention. – 18

Dillon Garris was born in 1975 in France and studied design and architecture at the Ecole Bleue. He has made a number of furniture prototypes to date. – 61

Mark Garside works for Inflate in London. – 130

Peter Gest is a product designer and decorator who works as part of Drop Design, a group of four independent designers from Sweden. – 196

Stefano Giovannoni was born in La Spezia, Italy, in 1954 and graduated from the architecture department at the University of Florence in 1978. From 1978 to 1990 he lectured and carried out research at Florence University and also taught at the Domus Academy in Milan and at the Institute of Design in Reggio Emilia. He is the founding member of King-Kong Production, which is concerned with avant-garde research in design, interiors, fashion and architecture. Clients include Alessi, Cappellini, Arredaesse and Tisca France. In 1991 he designed the Italian Pavilion at 'Les Capitales Européennes de Nouveau Design' exhibition, which was held at the Centre Georges Pompidou in Paris. – 51, 131, 210, 213

Ernesto Gismondi was born in 1931 in San Remo, Italy. He studied at Milan Polytechnic and the Higher School of Engineering, Rome. In 1959, with Sergio Mazza, he founded Artemide SpA, of which he is the president and managing director. Since 1970 he has designed various lights for Artemide. In 1981 he was involved in the development of Memphis. – 95

Konstantin Grcic was born in 1965 in Germany. He trained as a cabinet maker and continued his education at the John Makepeace School for Craftsmen, then studied design at the Royal College of Art, London, on a scholarship from Cassina. He worked in the studio of Jasper Morrison during 1990 and is currently working as a freelance furniture designer in London and Munich for companies including ClassiCon, Cappellini, Authentics, SCP, Montina, Flos and Plaza Design, Tokyo. Interior design projects include a private house in Bad Homburg and a presentation for Authentics at the Ambiente Fair in 1995 and at the Louvre, Paris in the same year. Since 1995 he has been professor of industrial design at the Hochschule in Bereich. – 67, 100

Monica Guggisberg and Philip Baldwin are an American/Swiss couple who have been working together for 15 years. They trained in Sweden at the Orrefors Glass School and later in the studio of Ann Wolff and Wilke Adolfsson. In 1982 they established their own design and hot glass studio near Lausanne in Switzerland. Their creations have been exhibited widely in Europe, America and Japan and are to be found in many museums. – 83

Alfredo Häberli was born in Buenos Aires in 1964 and studied industrial design at the Hochschule für Gestaltung in Zurich. He graduated in 1991 and in the same year started his collaboration with Christophe Marchand with a research grant from IKEA. They founded their own studio in 1993, and have since held over a hundred exhibitions. Clients include Alias, Driade, Luceplan, Authentics and Thonet. – 28, 72, 210

Isabel Hamm studied ceramic design in Germany, then from 1996 to 1998 studied for her Masters degree in Glass and Ceramics at the Royal College of Art in London. Before moving to London she had her own studio in Cologne and received commissions from Apple and Fairform. She is also involved in film and video work. – 106

Masako Hayashibe was born in 1940 in Tokyo. She studied history of religion in Stockholm, where she also became interested in textile weaving. In 1976 she returned to Japan and started the Spiral workshop. – 167

Sam Hecht was born in London in 1969. After studying at the Royal College of Art he worked as an interior and industrial designer. He moved to Tel Aviv and joined the Studia group, then moved to San Francisco where he began his collaboration with IDEO. He has since completed projects for AT&T and NEC as well as designing office interiors for IDEO. He now works for IDEO in Japan with clients such as NEC, Seiko and Matsushita. He won the D&AD Exhibition Category Award in 1998. He lectures in Japan and his work forms part of the permanent collection of the Museum of Modern Art. – 174, 177

Gerhard Heufler is a freelance industrial designer. He lectures on the design and ergonomics of electronic appliances at the Technical University in Graz, and is head of the FH College of Design, also in Graz. He has won five Austrian State Awards for Design and a Silver IDEA in 1998. – 192

Massimo Iosa Ghini was born in Borgo Tossignano, Italy, in 1959 and graduated in architecture from Milan Polytechnic. Before working with Ettore Sottsass and Memphis in 1986, he was involved in drawing cartoons for international magazines. In 1987 he launched his first collection, Dynamic, for Moroso which received awards worldwide. In 1991 he presented a collection of furniture that continued research he had been doing on the moulding of wood. Interior design projects include the planning of the fashion chain Fiorucci and the planning and design of the Renault Italy showrooms. Since 1992 he has held two major retrospectives, one at the Steininger Gallery, Munich and the second at the Inspiration Gallery in the Axis Building, Tokyo. Iosa Ghini is also involved in the design of eye-wear, consumer electronics, bathroom suites and illumination. In 1995 he was invited to an international congress of architects organized by IFI at Nagoya - the only Italian ever to be given this honour. He is a member of the ABN (Global Business Network). – 24

James Irvine was born in London in 1958 and graduated from the Royal Academy of Art in 1984. He then moved to Italy and worked as a consultant designer for Olivetti with Ettore Sottsass and Michele de Lucchi. He participated in ë12 New Memphis 86í and became a member of the group Solid. In 1987 Olivetti arranged a cultural exchange for Irvine with Toshiba in Tokyo, where he carried out research in industrial design. On his return to Milan he designed industrial products for Olivetti with Michele de Lucchi and was responsible for a new range of mini-computers and workstations. In 1988 he set up his own studio in Milan, designing interiors, furniture and industrial products and collaborating with companies including Alessi, Cappellini and Fantini. In 1990 Irvine was a visiting lecturer at the Domus Academy, Milan. He held his first personal exhibition at the Royal College of Art, London in 1993. – 16, 151

Hella Jongerius studied at the Eindhoven Academy of Industrial Design and spent periods as an apprentice with Xinta Tinta fashion fabrics in Barcelona and with Catherine Laget in Paris, training in styling. She has exhibited at Le Vent du Nord in Paris, at Droog Design in Milan and in the show ëMutant Materials in Contemporary Designí at the Museum of Modern Art, New York. – 43, 118

Patrick Jouin was born in Nantes, France, in 1967. He studied industrial design at ENSCI/Les Ateliers and has since worked with Philippe Starck during his collaboration with Thomson Multimedia and thereafter in Starck's studio. Designs developed as prototypes for VIA have now been manufactured by Ligne Roset, Cappellini, Facto and Fermob. – 147

Masakazu Kanatani has worked for Sony Corporation since 1986. In 1995 he was made responsible for the design of the MD Walkman. – 188

Peter Karpf was born in 1940 in Copenhagen. He worked as a carpenter before entering the Academy of Arts and Crafts in 1961 to study furniture design. He collaborated with the textile artist Nina Koppel, with furniture and industrial designer Grete Jalk and with the architect Arne Jacobsen. He has developed many furniture and lighting products, including a table and chair in laminated components which won a prize from the Copenhagen Cabinetmakers Guild in 1962; and the NXT 01 side chair which gained international acclaim and has been purchased by many leading design museums. In 1989 he wrote an architectural manifesto and formed the Alfabetica Group. Since 1986 he has been developing an alternative interior programme of furniture and lamp designs. – 34

Motomi Kawakami was born in Hyogo Prefecture in 1940. He graduated in industrial design from Tokyo National University of Fine Arts and Music, then worked with Angelo Mangiarotti in Milan before founding Kawakami Design Office. He is a lecturer at the design department of the Tokyo National and Aichi Prefectural Universities of Fine Arts and Music. He has taken part in exhibitions and won awards in Japan, most recently being the recipient of the Yokohama Civic Design Award (1996). – 178

David Khouri see Comma

Perry A. King and Santiago Miranda have worked together in MIlan since 1976 on industrial, interior, interface, and graphic design. In addition to collaborating with some of the main office furniture and lighting companies in Italy, King and Miranda have designed for manufacturers in the electromechanical and office equipment industries. Their interior design projects are to be found in Milan, Rome, Paris, London, Madrid and Tokyo. They designed the extèrior public lighting system for Seville Expo'92. – 92

Eero Koivisto – see Claesson Koivisto Rune

Defne Koz is a freelance industrial designer. She has been based in Milan since 1989 when she received her Masters degree from the Domus Academy. She worked for Sottsass Associati before becoming freelance and now designs electrical appliances, consumer electronics, furniture, home accessories, lighting systems, tableware, objects and the interiors of private houses and shops. She has held conferences and seminars at the Domus Academy as well as at the Istanbul Technical University, Turkey and the Architectural Association, London. – 196

Yrjö Kukkapuro was born in Wyborg, Finland, in 1933. He studied at the Institute of Crafts and Design from 1954 to 1958 and has run his own freelance agency since 1959. He was a teacher at the Helsinki Polytechnic, department of architecture, and at the University of Industrial Arts, Helsinki where he was rector until 1980 and artist/professor until 1993. He is well known throughout Scandinavia, having been honoured with prizes since the early 1960s. He received the Kaj Franck Design Award at the Design Forum in Finland in 1995. His work can be found in many museums, including the Museum of Modern Art, New York; the Victoria and Albert Museum, London; the Museum of Applied Art in Helsinki; the Israel Museum, Jerusalem; and the Vitra Design Museum, Weil am Rhein. – 51

Erik Jan Kwakkel was born in Delfzijl, The Netherlands, in 1965. He trained at the Hogeschool voor de Kunsten Arnhem, in the faculties of fine art and three-dimensional design. Since then he was worked as a jewellery designer and ceramicist. He has exhibited his work in The Netherlands and abroad, including 'Le Vent du Nord III' show in Paris and 'Dry Bathing' in Milan. He teaches ceramic design in various institutions in The Netherlands and in 1997 was appointed guest designer for a series of unique pieces at the crystal works of Royal Leerdam BV. – 128

Fons Labohm was born in 1940 in The Netherlands. He studied product design at the Design Academy, Eindhoven, and worked for 31 years at CID Consumer Electronics. He has worked for five years at Philips Lighting. – 103

Marta Laudani and Marco Romanelli work together as interior and product designers. Laudani graduated in Rome in 1979. Her competition project for the piazza in the Parco dei Caduti in Rome won first prize and executive status in 1990. Romanelli took a Masters degree in design after graduating in architecture in 1983. He worked for Mario Bellini until 1985 when he became freelance. He was editor at *Domus* magazine from 1986 to 1994 and has been a design editor at *Abitare* since 1995. He works as a consultant with Driade and is art director at Montina and Oluce. – 80

Olavi Lindén was born in Ekenas, Finland, in 1946. He is both an engineer and a designer. Since 1984 he has been product development manager at Fiskars Consumer Oy Ab. He has won many prizes for his work including the IF Design Award, Hanover in 1996, 1997 and 1998 for various garden pruners and loppers. – 201

Stefan Lindfors was born in the Aland archipelago between Sweden and Finland in 1962. He studied interior architecture and furniture design at the University of Art and Design in Helsinki and is currently active as a product designer and sculptor. In 1996 he was commissioned to design a sculpture (Winged Victory) for the Swatch Pavilion at the Olympic Games in Atlanta and also held an exhibition of sculpture at the Finnish Embassy in Washington DC entitled 'Freedom of Speech'. In 1992 Lindfors was the recipient of the most highly acclaimed Nordic cultural award, the Vaino Tanner 'Trailblazer'. He is the Joyce C. Hall distinguished professor of design and chair of the design department at the Kansas City Art Institute, and is a member of the Association of Finnish Interior Architects and the Association of Finnish Sculptors. – 140

Piero Lissoni was born in 1956. He studied architecture at Milan Polytechnic and then worked for G14 Studio, Molteni and Lema. With Nicoletta Canesi in 1984 he formed his own company, which is involved in product, graphic, interior and industrial design as well as architectural projects. Since 1986 he has worked with Boffi Cucine as art director, creating corporate images and sales outlets, and in 1987 began to collaborate with Porro, Living Design, Matteograssi and Iren Uffici. He worked in Japan in the early 1990s for the Takashimaya company. Since 1994 he has worked as art director for Lema and in 1995 became the art director for Cappellini and started his collaboration with Cassina and Nemo. In 1996 Lissoni was appointed art director for Units, the new Boffi and Cappellini kitchen company, and opened two showrooms in Paris for Matteograssi and Boffi. He was awarded the Compasso d'Oro in 1991 for the Esprit kitchen designed for Boffi. – 44

Ross Lovegrove was born in 1958 in Wales. He graduated from Manchester Polytechnic in 1980 with a Bachelor of Arts degree in industrial design, later receiving a Masters from the Royal College of Art, London. He has worked for various design consultancies including Allied International Designers, London and frogdesign in Germany. In 1984 he moved to Paris to work for Knoll International and became a member of the Atelier de Nîmes, a group of five designers which included Gérard Barrau, Jean Nouvel, Martine Bedin and Philippe Starck. In 1986 he co-founded Lovegrove and Brown Design Studio which was later replaced by Lovegrove Studio X. Clients include Louis Vuitton, Luceplan, Tag Heuer, Philips, Sony and Apple Computers. His work can be seen in major design collections, including the Museum of Modern Art, New York; the Guggenheim Museum, New York; the Axis Centre, Japan; the Centre Georges Pompidou in Paris and the Design Museum in London where, in 1993, he curated the first permanent collection. Lovegrove is a visiting lecturer at the Royal College of Art. – 79

Vico Magistretti was born in Milan in 1920 and graduated with a degree in architecture from Milan Polytechnic in 1945. Since 1967 he has been a member of the Academy of San Luca in Rome, as well as teaching at the Domus Academy in Milan. He is also an honorary member of the Royal College of Art in London, where he is a visiting professor. He has been the recipient of numerous major awards, including the Gold Medal at the Milan Triennale in 1951, the Compasso d'Oro in 1967 and 1979 and the Gold Medal of the Society of International Artists and Designers in 1986. Magistretti's buildings are primarily found in Italy, but his furniture, lamps and other designs are well known internationally. He has worked for companies including Alias, Artemide, Cassina, de Padova, Fiat, Knoll International and Rosenthal. – 23, 50, 64

Biographies

Angelo Mangiarotti was born in 1921 and lives and works in Milan. He graduated from Milan Polytechnic where he later taught architecture. He was visiting professor at the Design Institute of the Illinois Institute of Technology in Chicago in the 1950s. In 1955 he opened his own office with Bruno Morassutti, with whom he worked until 1960. In 1989, together with 12 Japanese architects and designers, he opened the Mangiarotti & Associates office in Tokyo. Among his more recent projects are the glasses First Glass and Ebbro, a series of crystal vases named after the four seasons, the steel service Ergonomica and the bookcase Ypsilon. Mangiarotti lectures in many universities throughout the world. He has received numerous awards, including the ADI Compasso d'Oro prize in 1994. – 60, 65

Christophe Marchand see Alfredo Häberli

Enzo Mari was born in Novara, Italy in 1932 and studied at the Academy of Fine Art in Milan. In 1963 he co-ordinated the Italian group Nuove Tendenze and in 1965 was responsible for the exhibition of optical, kinetic and programmed art at the Biennale in Zagreb. In 1972 he participated in 'Italy: the New Domestic Landscape' at the Museum of Modern Art, New York. Mari is occupied with town planning and teaching and has organized courses for the history of art department at the University of Parma and the architecture department at Milan Polytechnic. He has also lectured at various institutions including the Centre for Visual Communication in Parma and the Academy of Fine Arts in Carrara. He has been awarded the Compasso d'Oro on three occasions: for design research by an individual (1967); for the Delfina chair (1979); and for the Tonietta chair for Zanotta (1987). His work can be found in the collections of various contemporary art museums, including the Stedelijk Museum, Amsterdam, the Musée des Arts Décoratifs, Paris and the Kunstmuseum, Düsseldorf. Since 1993 he has collaborated with the KPM (Royal Porcelain Works) in Berlin, and in 1996 staged the 'Arbeiten in Berlin' exhibition at Charlottenburg Castle. – 126, 214

Alberto Meda was born in Como, Italy in 1945 and graduated with a degree in mechanical engineering from Milan Polytechnic in 1969. He worked at Magneti Marelli as assistant to the production manager, and at Kartell as an executive producer before starting a freelance practice collaborating with Gaggia, Kartell, Centrokappa, Lucetero, Cinelli, Fontana Arte, Luceplan, Aristolo, Mondadori, Mandarina Duck and Carlo Erba. He was awarded the Compasso d'Oro in 1989 for his Lola lamp and the Design Plus in 1992 for the Titania lamp. In 1994 he won the European Design Prize for his work with Luceplan and the Compasso d'Oro for the Metropoli series of lamps (again for Luceplan). In 1995 his chair LightLight was chosen for the Vitra exhibition '100 Masterpieces' at the Design Museum, London. Other exhibitions include the Milan Triennale in 1992, 'The Lightness' section in 'Il Giardino della Cose', 'Design, Miroir du Siècle' in Paris and 'Mutant Materials in Contemporary Design' at the Museum of Modern Art, New York in 1995. He lectures at both the Domus Academy and Milan Polytechnic. – 73, 90

Gioia Meller Marcovicz was born in Hamburg in 1955. She received her Masters degree in fashion design at the Modeschule in Munich and became a freelance fashion designer, working for Jaeger and Norman Hartnell as well as designing the stage clothes for the singer Sade. In 1991 she attended the Royal College of Art and was awarded the Princess of Wales Scholarship. She graduated with a Masters in furniture design in 1993. She has designed furniture for international companies and private clients including Issey Miyake. – 30

Thomas Meyerhöffer was born in Sweden and graduated from the Art Center College of Design in 1991. He is a founding principal of VOID (Virtual Office of Integrated Design) in San Francisco. Previously he designed for Julian Brown, Porsche, IDEO and Apple. His design awards include Best of Category/ID Magazine Annual Design Review, IF Awards and two British D&AD Silver Awards. The eMate is in the permanent collection of the Museum of Modern Art in New York. – 172

Santiago Miranda see Perry A. King

Shin Miyashita has worked for Sony Corporation since 1976 and is now designing for the personal video design group. – 184

Massimo Morozzi was born in Florence in 1941. Today he is an Associate of the CDM Group (Consulenti Design Milano) and develops co-ordinated image projects and product lines. Clients include Alessi, Cassina, Driade, Ham, Georgetti, Edra and Mazzei and he is currently developing designs for IRJ Corporate Image in Japan. Morozzi is art director of Edra and Mazzei. In 1990 he set up Morozzi and Partners with Silvia Centellegne, Giovanni Lauda and Cristina Dosio Morozzi. He lectures in Amsterdam, São Paulo, Melbourne and at the Domus Academy and the Istituto Europeo di Disegno in Milan. – 31

Ann Morsing and Beban Nord are the founder members of Box Architects and Box Möbler. Morsing was born in Uppsala, Sweden in 1956. She studied art in San Francisco and later took an art and craft course in the department of interior architecture at the Konstfackskolan, Stockholm. Beban Nord was born in Stockholm in 1956. She studied art history and fine art before enrolling in the interior architecture department of the Konstfackskolan. Together they have received the Forum Narmilo Prize for the best home furniture and the Golden Chair nomination for their interior design of an advertising agency in Sweden. – 64, 93

Mitsuhiro Nakamura joined Sony Corporation in 1983 and now works in their general audio design group. – 190

Jan Nemecek see Michal Fronek

Marc Newson was born in Sydney in 1963 and graduated from the Sydney College of Art in 1984. In 1985 the Powerhouse Museum in Sydney acquired some of his designs for its permanent collection, and at the same time offered him a Craft Council grant to devise new work. From 1987 Newson worked in Japan for Idee, creating amongst other designs, the Felt and Orgone chairs. After four years in Japan, Newson moved to Paris and worked for Cappellini, Flos and 3 Suisses. He developed the Glulim chair for Moroso and the Orgone glassware series for Progetto Oggetto, and designed a range of POD watches. He was named 'Designer of the Year' at the Salon du Meuble in Paris in 1993. In 1995 Newson started a series of interior design projects, including the Coast restaurant in London and other restaurant designs – Mash in Manchester and Osman in Cologne. Subsequent projects have included the Syn Studio in Tokyo and a chain of shops for Walter van Beirendonck W&LT. In 1997 Newson opened a studio in London and he is currently working on new designs and forthcoming exhibitions in New York and Los Angeles. – 59, 131, 194

Beban Nord see Ann Morsing

Katsuhiko Ogino was born in 1944 and graduated from the Musashino University of Art in 1966. From then until 1969 he was a lecturer at the Japan Design School after which he established various practices - Mono-Pro Kogei (1972), Humpty Dumpty Ltd (1976) and Time Studio Ltd (1978). In 1986 he was made a member of the Craft Centre, Japan, of which he is now director –

Katsuhiko Ogino was born in 1944 and graduated from the Musashino University of Art in 1966. Until 1969 he was a lecturer at the Japan Design School after which he established various practices - Mono-Pro Kogei (1972), Humpty Dumpty Ltd (1976) and Time Studio Ltd (1978). In 1986 he was made a member of the Craft Centre, Japan, of which he is now director. – 120

Olgoj Chorchoj see Michal Fronek and Jan Nemecek

ON Design is the studio of Klaus Nolting and Andreas Ostwald. Born in 1964 in Zürich and Lübeck respectively, the partners both studied at the Industrie-Design Fachhochschule in Kiel. ON Design collaborate with a number of companies, including ClassiCon, FSM Frank Sitzmöbel and Fritz Hansen. – 81

Roberto Palomba and Ludovica Serafini established their own design and architecture studio in 1994. Since then they have been responsible for the restoration of the historical gardens Caffarelli in Campidoglio, and Caroli in Largo Argentina. They have also worked on several hotel designs and the restructuring of the Nazareno Gabrielli shops in Monza and Pisa as well as the design of a series of new shops in Dubai. They are involved in set design for television and ballet productions, and urban planning, having recently completed the master plan for the new superfast electric bus from Casaletto to Piazza Venezia for the municipality of Rome. Palomba and Serafini act as art directors for numerous firms, including AllGlass, and as consultants for the corporate image and public relations of the Finnish sauna firm, Effegibi. – 110, 204

Roberto Pamio was born in Mestre, Venice in 1937. He studied architecture at the University of Venice and currently works in Venice and New York. As well as residential, commercial and industrial architecture, Pamio is also active in product and retail project design. He has won many design awards in Italy and abroad. His work has been exhibited in both solo and group shows at international centres and museums. – 81

Jorge Pensi is a Spanish architect and industrial designer born in 1946 in Buenos Aires, Argentina. He has worked in Barcelona since 1977, specializing in the design of furniture, lighting, fittings and product image. He has been associated with Perobell, the SIDI Group, Amat, Herrola & Lux and the magazine On Diseño. He has received acclaim for his designs, most notably the Toledo chair for which he was given the first Award Selection SIDI 1988, two silver Deltas and an Award Design Auswahl 90 from the Stuttgart Design Centre. He has lectured in Spain, England and the USA. – 48, 49, 55

Renzo Piano was born in Genoa in 1937. His buildings include the Centre Georges Pompidou in Paris (1977), the Nicaulla Stadium in Bari and the Kansai International Airport in Osaka. He has received many prizes and awards including the Compasso d'Oro, Erasmus and Kyoto awards. He is currently working on the overall layout – and eight of the buildings – of the Potsdamer Platz renovation in Berlin. – 138

Carl Pickering and Claudio Lazzarini have worked together since 1983. Their practice, Lazzarini Pickering Architects, is involved in architecture, re-use and restructuring, design and art direction in Italy and abroad. Pickering was born in 1960 in Sydney, he moved to Italy in 1980 and studied architecture at the University of Venice. Lazzarini was born in Rome in 1953 and graduated from La Sapienza University, establishing his practice in 1982. Recent projects include the conversion of a sixteenth century building in Prague into shops, offices and apartments, head offices in Rome for Fendi and Fendi boutiques in Rome and Venice. The practice has designed furniture for Aclimo ISL, its Isotropo furniture system was selected for the Compasso d'Oro prize in 1998. – 71

Udo Posch was born in 1951 in Limburg, Germany. He studied education and social sciences at the University of Marburg and, 10 years later industrial design at the University of Kassel. Today he works as a designer of furniture and industrial products. In the mid 1990s he founded his own company, Posch Glasform, now Posch Collection. – 109

Neil Poulton was born in 1963 in the UK. He studied industrial design technology at Napier University, Edinburgh, then gained a Masters degree from the Domus Academy in Milan in 1988. He is now based in Paris and designs products, lights and furniture for various companies in Europe and America. – 86

RADI Designers was founded by Florence Doléac Stadler, Laurent Massaloux, Olivier Sidet, Robert Stadler and Claudio Colucci. From 1994 to 1997 they practised in Paris, Vienna and Tokyo. Their office is now based in Paris with a branch in Tokyo, headed by Colucci who previously worked as a designer for Idee in Japan. Florence Stadler was a design consultant for Sommer Allibert until 1996. Massaloux and Sidet both worked for Philippe Starck in 1996 and than in the design department of Thomson Multimedia. Robert Stadler, who is of Austrian origin, was invited by Ron Arad to teach at the Academy of Applied Arts in Vienna where he worked from 1994 to 1997. RADI designers collaborate with the Kréo agency who presented their first exhibition at Emmanuel Perrotin's gallery in Paris in 1998. – 215

Karim Rashid graduated in industrial design from Carleton University in Ottawa, Canada in 1982. After graduate studies in Italy he moved to Milan for a one year scholarship in the studio of Rodolfo Bonetto. On his return to Canada he worked for seven years with KAN Industrial Designers in Toronto designing projects ranging from high-tech products to furniture and also designing the Babel and North clothing collections from 1985 to 1990. Today he is a full-time associate professor of industrial design at the University of Arts in Philadelphia. He has also taught at the Pratt Institute, the Rhode Island School of Design and Ontario College of Art. Since 1992 he has been principal designer for Karim Rashid Industrial Design in New York, designing products, lighting, tableware and furniture. He has won many awards including the Good Design Award/Permanent Collection (32 objects for Nambé Mills) in 1995 and ID 40 Leading Edge Designers from ID magazine in 1996. His work has been exhibited in the Museum of Modern Art, New York, The Chicago Athenaeum, and the Design Museum, London. – 54, 208

Paolo Rizzatto was born in Milan in 1941 and graduated in architecture from Milan Polytechnic. He founded Luceplan in 1978 with Riccardo Sarfatti, and from 1985 to 1987 he designed for Busnelli and Molteni and was also involved with interior architecture planning and exhibitions, and interior design for private residences. Today he works as a freelance designer. He has collaborated with many leading manufacturers and has exhibited his work worldwide. Examples can be seen in the permanent collection of the Museum of Modern Art in New York. In 1990 he was invited to Japan to represent Italian design in the exhibition 'Creatività' in Tokyo. He has been awarded the Compasso d'Oro on three occasions: in 1987 for his lamp D7, in 1989 for the Lola lamp series produced for Luceplan and in 1995 for the Metropoli lamp series, again for Luceplan. Rizzatto has taught at various university institutes including Columbia University in New York, Milan Polytechnic, Washington University in Saint Louis and the Cranbrook Academy of Art in Michigan. – 38, 73, 90

Vibeke Rohland studied art history at Copenhagen University, then worked at the Willumsen Museum of Art. From 1982 to 1986 she studied in the textile department of the Copenhagen School of Decorative Arts. In 1987 she started work for Eliakim Création de Tissus in Paris where she was responsible for the handpainting of textiles for haute couture and produced a textile collection for the Japanese market. Since 1991 she has been working on a freelance basis for Esprit in Düsseldorf and New York and Agnès B in Paris. Exhibitions to date have included 'Textile Manifestation' at the Museum of Decorative Arts, Denmark (1988); 'Dansk Design Aktuelt' (1992); and solo shows, most recently at the Borås Art Museum, Sweden (1998). In 1995 she was invited to design interiors and accessories for the Danish State Railway. – 145

Marco Romanelli see Marta Laudani

Paolo Romoli was born in Cascine, Italy and received his degree from the ISIA in Florence in 1965. In 1970 he founded the studio 'Metaform Industrial Design' with Sergio Baroncioni, Pier Angelo Cetica, Sergio de Clasicini and Sandro Zanni and today collaborates with Carlo Bimbi. He has taught model making at various design institutions and from 1972 to 1996 was professor of design in the Laboratory of Metallic Applications of the Istituto Statale d'Arte, Florence. Today he is also professor of model making at the ISIA. – 50

Aldo Rossi (1931–1998) was born in Milan and studied architecture at Milan Polytechnic. He began his career in 1956 working with Ignazio Gardella and later with Marco Zanuso. He established his own practice in 1959. From 1960 he was editor-in-chief of *Casabella*. He was appointed professor at Milan Polytechnic in 1965 and later at Venice University, and also taught in Zurich and the USA. In 1983 he was made director of the architecture section of the Venice Biennale. His many award-winning works include Modena Cemetery (1971); the Teatro del Mondo at the 1980 Venice Biennale; the School of Architecture, University of Miami (1989); and Hotel Il Palazzo, Fukuoka (1989). In 1987 he contributed to the Parc de la Villette in Paris and in 1989 designed the Centre d'Art Contemporain in Limousin, France. He designed numerous products for Alessi, most notably the 1986 Il Conico kettle. He also designed furniture for Molteni and Unifor. – 132

Ola Rune see Claesson Koivisto Rune

Rolf Sachs is a London-based designer. He studied business administration in London and San Francisco but his interest in art, design and film resulted in a career in furniture design. He has held one-man shows in Germany and has taken part in group exhibitions in Germany, Austria and Paris. – 109

Masatoshi Sakaegi was born in 1944 in Chiba-ken, Japan. In 1983 he founded the Masatoshi Sakaegi Design Studio, which specializes in ceramic and melamine tableware and ceramic sculpture. He has won many awards for his work, some at the 4th International Ceramics Competition 1995 in Mino, Japan. In 1997 he was selected as one of the ten world-famous designers of the 50th 'Premio Faenza', the international exhibition of contemporary ceramics in Faenza, Italy. – 129

Thomas Sandell was born in Jakobstad, Finland, in 1959 and started his architectural studies in 1981 at the KTH, Stockholm. He worked for Professor Jan Henriksson on competition projects as well as retail and domestic schemes, then set up his own practice in 1989. He has undertaken progressively larger commissions and in 1996 he took part in an invited competition to design the stadium in Stockholm for the 2004 Olympic games. Sandell designs furniture and products for clients such as Cappellini, B&B Italia, Garsnäs, Källemo and SCP. He has also designed exhibitions for the Centre Georges Pompidou, Paris, the Design Museum in London and the Kulturhuset in Stockholm. His work has been collected by museums in Sweden and by the Design Museum, London. Sandell is currently a guest lecturer at the Konstfackskolan in Stockholm and is also head teacher at the Beckmans School of Design. – 56

Mark Sanders trained as an engineer before moving into design. He now works as a freelance product designer and consultant as well as being a part-time tutor at the Imperial College and the Royal College of Art in London. In addition to his folding bicycle, The Strida, he has designed patient transporters that unfold into operating tables, and folding golf carts. – 202

Marta Sansoni was born in Florence in 1963 and graduated in architecture in 1990. As a designer she has worked with companies including Alessi, Cassetti, Flavia Bitossi and Vicano. – 212

Winfried Scheuer was born in Calw, Germany, in 1952. He worked as a trainee in the styling department of Mercedes-Benz in Sindelfingen before studying at the Royal College of Art, London from 1979 to 1981. He has worked in London as a self-employed industrial designer since 1986 and has exhibited his work at Documenta Kassel and the Luci Exhibition, Memphis, Milan. His clients include Authentics, Aero, Apple UK, Posch Glas Collection and Wilkhahn. He is a visiting lecturer at the Royal College of Art, the Hochschule der Künste, Berlin and Glasgow School of Art and Design. – 82

Wulf Schneider was born in 1943. He studied furniture construction and interior design at the State Academy of Visual Arts in Stuttgart. He has held management positions with a number of architectural practices. In 1976 he founded the 'Office for Design Concepts'. His activities cover environmental and interior design, consultancy for industrial and furniture companies, council housing planning, design development for buildings and furniture, and writing. – 39

Herbert H. Schultes was born in 1938. He studied engineering and design in Munich and from 1961 to 1967 was employed by Siemens AG. He is the founder of the industrial design course at the Advanced Technical College in Munich. In 1967 he co-founded the Schlagheck Schultes Design Company, whilst still maintaining his links with Siemens, becoming head of design in 1985. Schultes is a board member of the Industrie Forum Design in Hanover and the International Design Centre in Berlin. He is also chairman of the board and founder of the Design Centre in Munich. – 96

Lloyd Schwan studied sculpture at the Art Institute of Chicago. In 1984 he formed the company Godley-Schwan with his partner Lyn Godley. His designs have been described as functional art objects. – 70, 152

Carina Seth-Andersson was born in Stockholm in 1965. She studied glass and ceramic design and has exhibited her work throughout Scandinavia and at the Milan Triennale (1994); the 'Not so Simple' show in New York (1996); and the Victoria and Albert Museum, London (1997). In 1998 she was asked by the City of Stockholm – Cultural City of Europe in that year – to contribute a glass object to the 'Quite Simply' collection. – 141

Koji Shimobayashi was born in Okayama, Japan, in 1967. He graduated from the Musashino University of Art and joined Olympus Optical Co. Ltd in 1991 as an industrial designer working on cameras, microscopes, medical equipment and microcassette tape recorders. – 191

Sigla was founded by Marina Bani, Patrizia Scarzella and Marco Penati in 1994. The studio is active mainly in the design and engineering of industrial products. – 24

Pedro Silva Dias was born in 1963 and lives in Lisbon. He graduated in product design from the Escola Superior de Belas Artes in Lisbon and is currently working as a product designer with companies such as Loja da Atalaia, Proto Design and Casa de Cerca Art Centre. – 85

Michael Sodeau studied product design at Central Saint Martin's College of Art and Design. He was a founder partner of Inflate in 1995 but left in 1997 to set up a new partnership with Lisa Giuliani. He launched his first collection, Comfortable Living, in 1997. This consists of furniture and homeware which is now sold internationally. – 69, 150, 154

Andrew Stafford was born in the UK in 1965. He trained at Kingston Polytechnic and today works for clients such as SCP, Mitsubishi, Rogers International and Volvo. – 19

Philippe Starck was born in Paris in 1949 and trained at the Ecole Camondo in Paris. After a period of activity in New York he returned to France where he has since built up an international reputation. He has been responsible for major interior design schemes including François Mitterrand's apartment at the Elysée Palace, the Café Costes, and the Royalton and Paramount Hotels in New York. He has also created domestic and public multi-purpose buildings such as the headquarters of Asahi Beer in Tokyo, the Ecole Nationale Supérieure des Arts Décoratifs in Paris, and most recently the air traffic control tower for Bordeaux Airport. As a product designer he works for companies throughout the world, collaborating with Alessi, Baleri, Baum, Disform, Driade, Flos, Kartell, Rapsel, Up & Up, Vitra and Vuitton. From 1993 to 1996 he was worldwide artistic director for the Thomson Consumer Electronics Group. His many awards include the Grand Prix National de la Création Industrielle and his work can be seen in the permanent collections of all the major design museums. In 1997 he completed hotels in Miami and Los Angeles, and in 1998 the Canary Riverside hotel in London, a hotel in Bali, the restaurant in the Hilton hotel in Singapore and an incineration plant in Paris/Vitry. – 55, 88, 212

Christian Steiner was born in 1961 in Eisenstadt/Burgenland. He studied at the University of Applied Art in Vienna under Richard Sapper, Hermann Czech, Alessandro Mendini and Paolo Piva, and is currently a teacher there. – 47

Reiko Sudo was born in Ibaraki Prefecture, Japan, and educated at the Musashino University of Art. From 1975 to 1977 she assisted Professor Tanaka in the textile department. Before co-founding Nuno Corporation in 1984, she worked as a freelance textile designer and has since designed for the International Wool Secretariat, Paris and for the clothing company Threads, Tokyo. At present she is the director of Nuno Corporation and a lecturer at the Musashino University of Art. Her work can be seen in the permanent collections of the Museum of Modern Art and the Cooper-Hewitt National Design Museum, New York; the Museum of Art, Rhode Island School of Design; the Philadelphia Museum of Art; the Museum of Applied Arts, Helsinki; and the Musée des Arts Décoratifs, Montreal. Recent exhibitions include the 'Tokyo Creation Festival', Tokyo, 'The Textile Magician' show at the Israel Museum of Modern Art and 'Japanese Textile Design' at the Indira National Centre for Arts in India. She has received many prizes for her work, including the Roscoe Award in 1993 and 1994. – 160–63

Shinichi Sumikawa was born in Tokyo in 1962. He graduated from Chiba University industrial design department in 1984. He has worked for Sony both in America and Japan. Since becoming freelance in 1992 he has established Sumikawa Design and worked on communication tools, medical equipment, sports gear and miscellaneous product designs. In 1998 he was the winner of the Sapporo International Design Competition. – 199

Kaoru Sumita joined Sony Corporation as a designer in the audio group of the Corporate Design Centre. He has worked in the personal video department since 1986. – 185

Ilkka Suppanen was born in 1968 in Kotka, Finland. He studied in the department of architecture at Helsinki University, at the University of Art and Design, Helsinki and later at the Gerrit Rietveld Academy in Amsterdam. In 1995 he formed his own studio and since 1996 has taught at the Helsinki University of Art and Design. He exhibited at the Fifth International Exhibition of Architecture at the Venice Biennale, at the Island Gallery of Scandinavian Art in The Hague and in a touring exhibition from 1994 to 1995, which travelled throughout Europe, Japan, Taiwan and Korea. He also took part in the Snowcrash exhibition at the Facsimile Gallery during the Milan Furniture Fair in 1997 and at the Milan Satellite in 1998. His work is now manufactured by Cappellini. – 83

Martin Szekely was born in 1956 in Paris, where he now lives and works. He began to design furniture in 1979 and has won acclaim both in Europe and Israel. Though still active in the fields of furniture and interior design, he has diversified since 1991 into object and industrial design, creating jewellery boxes for Schatzl, crystal desk accessories for Swarovski, luggage for Delvaux and clocks for Hour Lavigne. He has exhibited his work both in France and abroad and examples can be seen in the permanent collections of numerous museums including the Musée des Arts Décoratifs, Paris; the Cooper-Hewitt National Design Museum, New York; the Israel Museum, Jerusalem; and the Kunstgewerbe Museums in Berlin and Cologne. In 1995 he took part in a travelling solo exhibition 'Around the World' which began at the Design Fair in Barcelona. Recent commissions include a chair for Montina International, the interior design of the Hôtel de Police in Rambouillet and a series of vases for the Museum of Vallauris. – 109

Renaud Thiry was born in 1968 in Paris. He graduated in industrial design from the ENSCI/Les Ateliers after having studied design and applied arts at De Monfort University in Leicester, England. Since 1995 he has been a freelance designer working for companies such as Ligne Roset, Habitat and Cinna, as well as producing two items himself under the name 'flandesign'. – 98

Timorous Beasties is a Glasgow-based design-led company specializing in interior textiles. Commissions range from fabrics and wallpaper for feature films and operas to specialist fabrics for interior designers. Their fabrics can be found in the collections of the Victoria and Albert Museum in London, the Cooper-Hewitt National Design Museum in New York and GOMA in Glasgow. –166

Biographies

Kazuhiko Tomita was born in Nagasaki, Japan, in 1965. He gained a B.Eng. in industrial design at Chiba University and in 1990 won a Cassina scholarship and British Council grant which enabled him to study furniture design at the Royal College of Art in London. The following year he was awarded first prize in the 'Architectural Future of Stainless Steel' competition judged by Sir Norman Foster. Later he was awarded the MA RCA Marchiette Award for his degree work 'Hadaka-no Piano, aria'. He has exhibited frequently at the Milan Furniture Fair as well as Abitare il Tempo. – 119, 123

John Tree has worked for Sony UK, European Design Centre since 1995. – 179

Takahiro Tsuge started working for Sony Corporation Corporate Design Centre in 1989 where he was responsible for the design of television equipment. He has now moved to the design centre of Sony America. – 190

Patricia Urquiola was born in Oviedo, Spain, in 1961 and today lives and works in Milan. She studied in the architecture department of Madrid University and at Milan Polytechnic where she graduated in 1989 under Achille Castiglioni; from 1990 to 1992 she assisted him and Eugenio Bettinelli at the polytechnic and the ENSCI in Paris. Until 1996 she also worked for De Padova, collaborating with Vico Magistretti. She founded her own studio in 1993 (with E. Ramerino and M. de Renzio), designing furniture and interiors. Since 1996 she has been a design consultant in the Lissoni Associati Studio where she collaborates with companies including Cappellini and Cassina. – 22

Patrick van de Voorde was born in 1961 in Belgium. He graduated in electro-mechanical engineering and has worked for 13 years on the development of CFL Lamps for Philips Lighting. – 103

Dick van Hoff was born in Amsterdam in 1971. He trained as a building worker and window dresser before studying three-dimensional design at the Hogeschool voor de Kunsten in Arnhem. In 1995 his tap Stop kraan was taken up by Droog Design and he has since had several other pieces developed by them and DMD as well as Rosenthal and United Colours of Benetton. – 122

Maarten Van Severen is an interior and furniture designer. He is mainly active in the design of small-scale domestic and retail schemes and has recently completed the Maison a Floirac with the architect Rem Koolhaas. His furniture and lighting designs have been in production since 1997 and he now works for clients such as Vitra, Switzerland, U-line Lighting and Target Lighting in Belgium. He has exhibited his work in group shows throughout Europe. In 1998 he received the IF Design Award, Hanover for U-line. In the same year he received the Flemish government's design prize. He is a visiting professor at the Academy of Fine Arts in Maastricht. – 94

Eugène van Veldhoven graduated from the Academy of Art and Architecture in Rotterdam in 1993, where he studied fashion and textile design. His clients include the fashion designers Marithe and François Girbaud in Milan, Bureau Edelkoort and Promostyl in Paris and the fashion magazine Vies. He has also designed a series of fabrics for use as woven wallcoverings for Vescom in Deurne. Recent projects include a collection of treated fabrics for ITS Artea in Milan. – 164

José Viana was born in 1960 and lives in Lisbon. He graduated in product design from the Escola Superior de Belas Artes in Lisbon and is now senior designer at Proto Design. He works as a freelance designer for companies such as Portugal Telecom, TV Cabo and Vegatron. – 100

Arnout Visser studied at the Art School in Arnhem, The Netherlands, from 1984 to 1989, then at the Domus Academy, Milan in 1990. Since then he has been working as a freelance designer in Arnhem, specializing in glass and ceramics. – 108, 128

Pia Wallén was born in Sweden in 1957. She was educated at Beckmans School of Design in Stockholm and has since exhibited her textile works throughout the world. Examples can be seen in various permanent museum collections including the Victoria and Albert Museum, London. She produced a felt collection for Progetto Oggetto Cappellini in 1992 and has been commissioned by the Museum of Modern Art in Sweden to design a curtain for their cinema. She has been producing carpets for Asplund since 1994. – 155, 156

Marcel Wanders graduated in product design from the Art Academy in Arnhem in 1988, by which time he had worked with Artifort and been awarded the Nestlé Design Prize. He was one of the founder members of WAAC Design and Consultancy, working with companies such as KLM, Swatch and Apple. In 1995 he opened his own studio, Wanders Wonders, and has broadened his client portfolio to include Cappellini, Rosenthal and British Airways. His work can be found in the permanent collections of the Stedelijk Museum, Amsterdam and the Museum of Modern Art in New York. – 27, 97, 112, 113, 121

Hans Peter Weidemann was born in 1958. He studied at the Hochschule für Gestaltung in Basle, and has been working as a furniture and lighting designer since 1986. That same year he took part in the exhibition 'Mobilier Suisse: Creation, invention' at the Centre Georges Pompidou, Paris. Since 1991 he has been designing for Atelier and from 1995 for Oluce. In 1991 he was awarded the Design Preis Schweiz. – 98

Ingrid Wiendels studied at the Eindhoven Design Academy under Ulf Moritz and graduated in 1997. Currently, she works on a freelance basis for the designer Paul Alexander Linse, for Fetim Ltd where she is a trends consultant and for Keja Donia BBDO Group. – 216–19

Wogg was founded in Switzerland in 1983 by Willi and Otto Glaser. Its aim was to develop a furniture collection using the existing production facilities of the carpentry firm Glaser AG, which was formed by their grandfather in 1898. The company works with designers such as Hans Eicheberger, Ludwig Roner, Ubald Klug and Gerd Lange. – 72, 74

Terence Woodgate was born in London in 1953. He studied at Westminster and Middlesex colleges and in the mid-1980s spent two years at what is now known as the London Guildhall University. His work consists mainly of furniture, lighting and product design. His clients include Cappellini, Casas, Concord Lighting, Punt Mobles, SCP, Teunen and Teunen and Victoria Design. He has won two major design awards: the British Design Award, 1992 and the German Design Award, Die Besten der Besten Design Innovation 1992. His work is exhibited in the collection of the Museum of Decorative Arts, Barcelona, and in the review collection of the Design Museum, London. In 1994 he set up a studio in Portugal and in 1996 a studio in Sussex, England. – 40

Yoshinori Yamada joined Sony Corporation in 1991, moving to their UK Design Centre in 1995. – 179

Hiroyuki Yamakado was born in Japan but has been living in France since 1977. He set up his own furniture design studio in 1986. – 99

Michael Young was born in Sunderland, England in 1966. He graduated from Kingston University in 1992 and established MY022 four years later. He has held one man shows throughout Europe as well as in Japan, and examples of his designs can be found in the Fondation National d'Art Contemporain, Paris; the Atelier des Enfants at the Centre Georges Pompidou, Paris and the Design Museum in London. – 41, 132

Yasuo Yuyama started working for Sony Corporation in their Corporate Design Centre in 1991 and is now responsible for designing personal audio and visual equipment. – 190

Massimo Zucchi graduated from the University of Rome in 1975. He is an architect and silversmith as well as professor of jewellery design at the Istituto Europeo di Disegno in Milan and Rome. He has held exhibitions of his silverware at many venues throughout Italy, most recently at the Collection Mac'93 at the Museum of Silver in Sartirana in 1995. – 133

Acquisitions by design collections in 1998.
Dates given in parentheses refer to the dates of the designs (from 1960 to the present day).

Australia
Powerhouse Museum, Sydney, New South Wales

Tableware
Alvar Aalto, vase, Aalto (c. 1997), manufactured by Iittala
Alvar Aalto, vase, Anniversary (1996), manufactured by Iittala
Bottle, Unravelled, blown by Benjamin Edols, wheel-cut by Benjamin Edols and Kathy Elliott (1997)
Bowl, Octopus, blown by Benjamin Edols, wheel-cut by Kathy Elliott (1996)
Zaha Hadid, tea and coffee set (4 pieces) (1997), manufactured by Sawaya and Moroni SpA
Shoji Hamada, vase (c. 1965)
Shoji Hamada, bowl (1970s)
Ulla Procope, tableware, Ruska range (7 pieces) (c. 1997), manufactured by Arabia
Lucie Rie, vase (1970s)
Lucie Rie, tea set (c. 1970)
Timo Sarpaneva, vase, Marcel (c. 1997), manufactured by Iittala
Borek Sipek, tea set, Service Semaine (incomplete), includes fruit bowl Dimanche, sugar bowl Vendredi, cake plate Lundi, teacup Mercredi (1990), Manufacture Nationale de Sèvres
Sandra Taylor, platter, The Meaning of Life (1994)
Kati Tuominen-Niittylä, jugs (2), Storybirds series, small jug Olga, large jug Oliver (1997), manufactured by Arabia
Tapio Wirkkala, jug, tumbler and plate, Ultima Thule series (c. 1997), manufactured by Iittala
Fujiwara Yu, two vases (1970s)
Fujiwara Yu, bowl (1970s)

Textiles
Glory Gnale, textile length (1997), made at the Powerhouse Museum, Sydney
Keasi (Lui), quilt, All the Colours Bloom in the Spring or Almost 8888 Trapeziums (1990)
Elsje King, wall hanging, Spinifex Stitching (1997)
Barbara Macey, quilt, Blue Maze Quilt (1987)
Rosie Pwerle, textile length (1997), made at the Powerhouse Museum, Sydney

Canada
Musée des Arts Décoratifs de Montréal

Furniture
Andrea Branzi, bookshelf, Wireless (1996)
Enzo Mari, chair, Box (1976)
Gaetano Pesce, chair, Dalila I (1980)
Ettore Sottsass, cabinet, Di Famiglia (1985)
Ali Tayar, shelving system, Ellen's Brackets (1993)

Lighting
Sergio Asti, lamp, Daruma (1966–68)
Andrea Branzi, lamp, Wireless (1996)
Alberto Meda and Paolo Rizzatto, lamp, Lola (1987)
Alessandro Mendini, lamp, Atomana (1984)
Eleonore Peduzzi-Riva, lamp, Molla (1971)
Gaetano Pesce, standing lamp, Rag no. 4 (1997)
Gaetano Pesce, wall light, Rag Round (1997)
Gaetano Pesce, lamp, Spaghetti (1997)
Franco Raggi, lamp, Velo (1987)

Tableware
Sergio Asti, cutlery, Boca (1973–75)
Gaetano Pesce, vase, Amazonia III (1997)
Gaetano Pesce, vase, Sant Ivo (1997)
Gaetano Pesce, vase, Spaghetti (1997)
Carlo Scarpa, jug (c. 1970)
Jane Timberlake, service, Wild Mannered (1994)
Masanori Umeda, set of vases, Yantra IT (1995)

Textiles
Gretchen Bellinger, fabrics, Spread Your Wings™ (1996); Stick Your Neck Out™ (1995); Casting Illusions™ (1990); Courting Cranes™ (1992); Golden Apples™ (1992); Queen Bee™ (1989); Pearly Gates™ (1997); Bubble Dot™ (1991); On The Right Track™ (1994); Isadora® (1981); Starry Night™ (1989); Stepping Out (1989); Pillow Talk™ (1995); Wigwam™ (1987)
Alessandro Mendini, rug, Oriented (1980)
Lori Weitzner, fabrics, Jacob's Ladder (1993); Solace (1993); Luminescence (1994)

Products
Sergio Asti, coffeepot (1989–90)
Sergio Asti, clock, Nuvola (1990–91)
Constantin Boym, plastic containers (1995)
Gaetano Pesce, basket, Tutti Frutti (1996)

Denmark
The Danish Museum of Decorative Art, Copenhagen

Lighting
Lars Eijers, brass lamp, Filosoflampe (1997)

Textiles
Jette Gemsøe, rug, Skibet Dannebrog (1997)
Jette Gemsøe, rug, Schakenborg (1997)
Louise Sass, printed fabric, Lineær Stak (1997)

Products
Nicolas Nicolaou, wristwatch (1997)
Nicolas Nicolaou, thermos, Furo (1997)
Nicolas Nicolaou, barbecue stander (1997)

France
Musée des Arts Décoratifs, Paris

Furniture
Guy de Rougemont, coffee table, Cloud (1970)
Olivier Leblois, set of cardboard furniture: armchair, FC (1993); armchair, T 41 (1995); child's armchair, FCE (1994); chair, Zig (1994), manufactured by Quart de Poil

Lighting
Verner Panton, Wire Lamp (1969)

Tableware
Laura de Santillana, dish, Seagold (1996), one-off
Laura de Santillana, 5 vases, Bamboo (1996), manufactured by Arcade
Robert Deblander, vase (1997), one-off
Francine Del Pierre, bowl (1967) and dish (1966)
Bruno d'Enfert, coffee set (1970–71), manufactured by Ravinet d'Enfert
Tom Dixon, vase, Double-buble (1994)
Elisabeth Fritsch, vase, Double Fault (1987), one-off
Anna Gili, vase, Profili (1997), manufactured by Salviati
Johanna Grawunder, 8 glasses from Bassonieu set (1996), manufactured by Salviati
Chris Knight, Spiked Bowl # 2 (1997)
Chris Knight, salt and pepper mills (1994)
Chris Knight, 2 tequila glasses, Spiking the Sun (1996)
Chris Knight, Corked Flask (1994)
Floris Meydam, vase, Diabolo from the Apollo series (1972), manufactured by Leerdam
Massimo Nordio, vase, Opposti series, (1997), one-off
Michael Rowe, vessel no. 24 (1994), vessel no. 26 (1995)
Scott Slagerman, vase, Fireworks series (1997), limited batch production
Martin Szekely, Perrier glass (1997)
Oscar Tusquets, canteen, 10 items (1995), manufactured by Driade SpA
Lyn Utzon, cup and saucer (1978), plate (1979), vase (1985)
Claude Varlan, vase (1997), one-off
Massimo and Lella Vignelli, knife and fork (1990), manufactured by sté Couzon

Products
Claude Bouchard, kettle (1997)
Tessa Clegg, secret box (1996)
Pucci de Rossi, Mobile Metafisico (1990–91)
Erik Dietman, 3 sculptures, La nuit de l'épine dorsale, Bunny O'Tool and Nénuphar maudit
Sylvain Dubuisson, tray, Réflexion polie, edited by Guy Degrenne (1996)
Philippe Hiquily, guéridon (1960s)
Richard Meitner, glass object, Karl (1997)
Marc Newson, Mistery clock (1986)
Gaetano Pesce, clock, Fish Design (1996)
Borek Sipek, tray (1995–97), manufactured by Driade SpA
Martin Szekely, clock, Marianne (1992–3), manufactured by Hour Lavigne
Didier Tisseyre, object-sculpture (1991)

Germany
Kunstmuseum Düsseldorf im Ehrenhof

Quasar Khan, chair, Angleterre (1968–9), manufactured by Rees, Stein & Co.
Verner Panton for Louis Poulsen, 3 flowerpot lamps

Vitra Design Museum, Weil am Rhein

Furniture
Cini Boeri, Serpentone (1971), manufactured by Arflex
Antonio Citterio, sofa, Diesis
Joe Colombo, 2 lounge chairs, Living-Center
Joe Colombo, bar stool, Birillo
De Pas/D'Urbino/Lomazzi, shelves, Longato (1970)
F. Druot, bench
Frank Gehry, 3 stacking chairs, Easy Edges
Group G14, armchair, Fiocco (1970), for Industrie Busnelli
Richard Hutten, chair-table
Enzo Mari, experimental chair (1973)
Xavier Matégot, armchair M3
Xavier Matégot, armchair M3, prototype
Marc Newson, chair, Embryo
Gio Ponti, desk, Apta (1970)
Marcel Wanders, Soft Knotted chair

Lighting
A. Brekveld, lamp, DMD 18
R. Graumans, lamp, DMD 08
Verner Panton, Pantower
Verner Panton, 3 lamps, Pan-Top
Tejo Remi, lamp, DMD 04

The Netherlands
Stedelijk Museum, Amsterdam

Furniture
Riccardo Blumer, chair, Laleggera (1996), manufactured by Alias srl
Wolf Brinkman, cupboard, Slappe Kast (1996), limited batch production
Bob Copray and Stefan Scholten, Chair Nr. 2 (1997), prototype
Bob Copray and Stefan Scholten, Chair Nr. 3 (1997), prototype
Frans de la Haye, chair, Centennial (1996), manufactured by Ahrend
Peter Ghyczy, chair, Garden Egg (1968), manufactured by Reuter Products
Giorgio Gurioli, chair, Joy (1997), manufactured by Acerbis International SpA
Ineke Hans, 2 chairs, Eat Your Heart Out (1997), limited batch production
Yrjö Kukkapuro, easy chair, Karuselli 412 and footstool (1964–5), manufactured by Haimi
Wittox & Knip, Design for a Table (1997), limited batch production

Lighting
Ingo Maurer, lamps, Zero One (1990); Eclipselipse (1989); Bibibibi (1982); Fukushu (1984); Hot Achille (1994); Lucellino (1992); Don Quixote (1989), manufactured by Ingo Maurer GmbH
Tsur Reshet, lamp, ASA 100 (1997)
Ettore Sottsass, lamp, Ashoka (1981), manufactured by Memphis
Frans van Nieuwenborg, lamp, The Saint (1998)

Products
Flex development, clock, Nine o'Clock (1995), manufactured by DMD

Norway
The Oslo Museum of Applied Art

Furniture
Eero Aarnio, table, Kantarelli (1969), manufactured by Asko
Luigi Colano, child's chair (1972), manufactured by Top System

Tableware
Kathinka Dysthe, mug and small and large plates for Frognerseteren Restaurant, Oslo (1996–7), manufactured by Porsgrunds Porselensfabrik
Walter Gropius and M.C. Millen, tea set (1969), manufactured by Rosenthal AG
Svein E. Juhlin, sugar and cream set (1991), manufactured by Dynoplast A/S
Grete Rønning, mug (1996), manufactured by Porsgrunds Porselensfabrik
Lise Sjåk-Bræk, mug (1996), manufactured by Porsgrunds Porselensfabrik

Products
Tormod Alnæs, picnic set (1972–77), manufactured by Møller Crates
Lotta Horn, dishwashing brush (c. 1980), manufactured by Kron A/S
Sigurd Persson, various brushes for dishwashing, nails etc. (1985), manufactured by Kron A/S
Grete Rønning, mug designed for the Lillehammer Olympics (1994), manufactured by Porsgrunds Porselensfabrik

National Museum of Decorative Arts, Trondheim

Braun iron, type 4332 (1980s)
Birgit Kaas Dahlgren, printed piece goods, Flight (1982), manufactured by Sandvika Veveri A/S

Sweden
Nationalmuseum, Stockholm

Lena Bergström, glass, Obelix (1997), manufactured by Orrefors – Kosta Boda AB
Erika Lagerbielke, glass, Intermezzo (1985), manufactured by Orrefors – Kosta Boda AB, Sweden
Erika Lagerbielke, glass, Merlot (1995), manufactured by Orrefors – Kosta Boda AB
Bruno Mathsson, chair, Kerstin (1979), manufactured by Dux Industrier
Anne Nilsson, glass, Zephyr (1996), manufactured by Orrefors – Kosta Boda AB

Röhsska Museet, Gothenburg

Furniture
Eero Aarnio, armchair (1998)
Sven Dalsgaard, chair (1990s), manufactured by Källemo
Peter Opsvik, child's chair, Tripp Trapp (1972)

Tableware
Anna Brogren, cup and saucer (1996)
Carlsson & Broman, bottle, Absolut vodka (1977–8)
Ann-Sofie Gelfius, 3 cups and saucers (1987, 1996, 1997)
Theresia Hvorsley, vase (1990s)
Ingela Karlsson, 3 bowls, Cafe Olé (1995)
Ingela Karlsson, 2 cups and saucers, French Lily (1991)
Bo Klevert, bowl (1997)
Stig Lindberg, coffee cups and saucers, Birka (1973), Berså (1960), Linda (1974), manufactured by Gustavsberg
Åsa Lindström, 2 goblets (1996)
Pia Rönndahl, coffee cup and saucer (1985), manufactured by Gustavsberg
Gunnel Sahlin, bottle, Swedish brandy (1997)
Thomas Sandell, 2 glasses for café au lait (1996), manufactured by Reijmyre Glassworks
Bengt Serenander, coffee cup and saucer, Jasmin (1971), manufactured by Gustavsberg
Agneta Spångberg, 4 cups and saucers (1991)
Mutsumi Suzuki, wine jar with sake drinking cup (1996)

Textiles
Gunila Axén, fabric, Galleri (1994)

Products
Konstantin Grcic, wastepaper basket, Square (1994), manufactured by Authentics
Gunilla Kihlgren, glass object (1995)
Richard Lindh, flower pot with saucer (1963), manufactured by Arabia
Rigmor Roxner, monumental bowl (1997)
Oiva Toikka, glass object, Tree (1990s)
Kennet Williamsson, three Blue berry baskets (1997)

228

Acquisitions

Switzerland
Museum für Gestaltung, Zurich

UK
The Design Museum, London

Victoria and Albert Museum, London

USA
Museum of Fine Arts, Boston, Massachusetts

Brooklyn Museum of Art, New York

The Chicago Athenaeum, The Museum of Architecture and Design, Chicago, Illinois

Philippe Starck, vacuum jug, Hot Fredo (1996), manufactured by alfi Zitzmann GmbH
Philippe Starck, spectacles, Starck Eyes (1996), manufactured by Alain Mikli International
Philippe Starck, Starck WashMobil Lavatory (1990), manufactured by Rapsel SpA
Philippe Starck, tray, Voilà Voilà (1992); kettle, Hot Bertaa (1990–91); lemon squeezer, Juicy Salif (1990–91), manufactured by Alessi SpA
Stuart Karten Design, Belkin computer cables (1995), manufactured by Belkin Components
Studio Red, Fujitsu Milan Pentium Pro Notebook Computer (1996), manufactured by Fujitsu Personal Systems
Matteo Thun, Trylogya Sanitary Fixtures (1998), manufactured by Santari Pozzi SpA
Tres Design Group Inc, Heart rate monitor watch/Series 3 and Series 5 (1996), manufactured by Sports Instruments USA inc
Antoine Volanis, bathroom scale, Slimmer (1996), manufactured by T-Fal Corporation
Michael Wagenhöfer, SieMatic Modula Kitchen (1995), manufactured by SieMatic Möbelwerke GmbH & Co. KG
Hannes Wettstein, wristwatch, V-Tronic (1997), manufactured by Ventura Design on Time SA
Yamaha Product Design Laboratory, silent violin (SV-100) (1997); silent session drum (DTX) (1996), manufactured by Yamaha Corporation
yellow circle, fountain pen and ball point pen, Pelikan Level L5 (1997), manufactured by Pelikan Vertriebsgesellschaft mbH
Nicole Zeller, BBQtensils (1997), manufactured by Zelco Industries Inc.

The Cooper-Hewitt National Design Museum, Smithsonian Institution, New York

Furniture
Donald Chadwick and William Stumpf, Aeron Chair (1992), manufactured by Herman Miller, Inc.
Dan Friedman, USA table (1993), manufactured by Neotu
David Kawecki, Puzzle Chair (1991), manufactured by 3D: Interiors
Bashir Zivari, stools, Kin-der-Link (1993), manufactured by Skools, Inc.

Lighting
Dan Friedman, floor lamp (c. 1987)
Henk Stallinga, light fixture, Watt (1995)

Tableware
Morison S. Cousins, flower arranger/vase (1996), manufactured by the Tupperware Corporation
Gerald Gulotta, five-piece flatware setting, Eros (1996), manufactured by Sasaki
Michael Schneider, flatware, Tools (1990s), manufactured by Mono
Henk Stallinga, bowl, Slab (1995)
Mark P. Wilson, MpW Design, ergonomic flatware, Flamingo (1996), manufactured by Curware

Products
Burton Rubin, ballpoint pen, evo pen (1993), manufactured by evo.pen, Inc.
Ergonomi Design Gruppen, Universal Turner/Handle (1990s)
frogdesign inc., Macintosh Personal Computer (1984), manufactured by Apple Computer
Jack Hokanson, razors, Spike (1996); Pudgy (1993); Stinger (1993); Wally (1993), manufactured by Hoke 2
George Nelson Associates, Daniel J. Lewis, Lexis-Nexis UBIQ Terminal (1979), manufactured by Lexis-Nexis
Zvi Yemini, toolbox, Tuff Stuff (1994), manufactured by ZAG Industries, Ltd

The Denver Art Museum, Denver, Colorado

Furniture
Gae Aulenti, chair, No. 4854 (1968)
Derek Davis, cabinet (c. 1985)
Arata Isozaki, chair, Marilyn (1972)
Vico Magistretti, chair, Gaudi (1970)
Enzo Mari, chair, Box (1976)
Jasper Morrison, chair, Ply-Chair (1989)
Pierre Paulin, lounge chair (1968)
Ettore Sottsass, bookcase, ES-4 (1993)
Shigeru Uchida, chairs, Okazaki (1996), Rattan (1974) and September (1977)
Masanori Umeda, chair, Getsuen (1998)

Robert Venturi, chairs, Deco 665 (1979–84) and Sheraton 664 (1979–84)

Lighting
Mario Botta, table lamp, Shogun (1986)
Tom Dixon, floor lamp/stool, Jack (1997)
Masayuki Kurokawa, table lamp, Domani (1976)
Masanori Umeda, lamp, Umeda Stand (1986)

Tableware
Michele de Lucchi, candlestick, CO12 MC SA (1990)
Michele de Lucchi, vases, MDL-8 (1993) and Vaso Bianco (1990)
Ludovico de Santillana, moulded glass vase (c. 1969)
Marco Ferreri, centrepiece, Antipodi (1996)
Johanna Grawunder, vase, JG-4 (1993)
Masayuki Kurokawa, cutlery, CU-B1, CU-B2, CU-B3 and CU-B4 (1998)
Masayuki Kurokawa, glass tumblers, GL-A1, GL-A2 and GL-A3 (1998)
Ettore Sottsass, vases, Mirto 111 (1997) and Mirto 112 (1997)
Masanori Umeda, tableware, Startray (1985)
Masanori Umeda, tea set, Mutsugoro (1985)
Masanori Umeda, vases, Yantra (1997) and Yantra C (1997)
Massimo Vignelli, dinnerware, Max (1964)

Products
Masayuki Kurokawa, wall clock, CFB (1973–83)
Masayuki Kurokawa, watch, Rabat (1987)
Ettore Sottsass, calculator, Summa 19 (1970)
Ettore Sottsass, table mirror, ES-3 (1993)
Shigeru Uchida, clock, Dear Morris (1989)
Marco Zanuso, bottle openers, MZ-1, MZ-2 and MZ-3 (1993)
Marco Zanuso, wooden chests, MZ-4 and MZ-7 (1993)

Los Angeles County Museum of Art, California

Furniture
Eugenia Butler, chair, Gris (1986)
Elsie Crawford, Joint (c. 1974), made by David Edberg
Elsie Crawford, Model Settee (c. 1974), made by David Edberg, prototype
Elsie Crawford, bookcase (c. 1974), made by David Edberg
Elsie Crawford, coffee table (reproduced 1997), made by David Edberg
Robert Ebendorf, pair of Green and Green chairs (1992)

Tableware
Robert Wilhite, untitled serving spoon and fork

Products
Elsie Crawford, Zipper Light I and II (1965)
Gere Kavanaugh, Umbrella (1967)

Metropolitan Museum of Art, New York

Morison S. Cousins, bowl (1997), manufactured by the Tupperware Corporation
Frank Gehry, armchair, Cross Check (1989–92)
Ettore Sottsass, armchair, Miss, Don't You Like Caviar (1987)
Ettore Sottsass, room divider, Carleton (1981)

Museum of Modern Art, New York

Furniture
Werner Aisslinger, chair, Juli (1996), manufactured by Cappellini SpA
Wendell Castle, chair, Molar (1968), manufactured by Northern Plastic
Antonio Citterio and Glen Oliver Löw, folding extension table, Battista (1991), manufactured by Kartell SpA
Tom Dixon, chair, S (1991), manufactured by Cappellini SpA
Toshiyuki Kita, The Multilingual Chair (1991), manufactured by Kotobuki Corporation
Shiro Kuramata, chair, Miss Blanche (1989), manufactured by Ishimaru Co.
MAP International, Christopher Connell, chair, Pepe (1992), manufactured by MAP (Merchants of Australian Products Pty, Ltd)
Enzo Mari, chair, Sof-sof (1971), manufactured by Driade SpA
Alberto Meda, chaise longue, Long frame (1994), manufactured by Alias srl
Jasper Morrison, chair, Lima (1995), manufactured by Cappellini SpA
Marc Newson, chaise longue, Orgone (1989), manufactured by Cappellini SpA
Marc Newson, chair, Wood (1988), manufactured by Cappellini SpA

Lighting
Harry Allen, lighting fixtures, Tower 1, Tower 2, Twist, Table lamp (1994), manufactured by Harry Allen and Associates
Sebastian Bergne, lighting fixture, Lamp Shade 1 (1991), manufactured by Radius GmbH
Joseph Forakis, hanging lighting fixture, Havana (1993), manufactured by Foscarini Murano SpA
Lyn Godley and Lloyd Schwan, lamp, Crinkle (1996), manufactured by Godley Schwan
Arik Levy, lamp, Need (1996), manufactured by L Design

Tableware
Takeshi Ishiguro, salt and pepper shakers, Rice (1994), prototype
Timo Sarpaneva, plate (1960s)

Textiles
Kaneko Orimono Co. Ltd, company design, roving weft fabric (1995–6), manufactured by Kaneko Orimono Co. Ltd

Products
Santina Bonini and Ernesto Spicciolato, bathroom accessories (box, cotton wool box, soap holder, toothbrush holder), Arctic Series (1994), manufactured by Gedy SpA
Constantin Boym and Laurene Leon Boym, containers, USE IT (1995), manufactured by Authentics artipresent GmbH
Claudio Cesar, ChromaFusion® (1988), manufactured by Cesar Color Inc.
Claudio Cesar, ChromaScreen™ (1988), manufactured by Cesar Color Inc.
Antonio Citterio and Glen Oliver Löw, container system, Mobil (1993), manufactured by Kartell SpA
Richard Feinbloom and Gordon Randall Perry, hand-held magnifiers, ClearVision II (1997), manufactured by Designs for Vision Inc.
Flex Development BV, Cable Turtle (1996), manufactured by Cleverline
Giorgio Gurioli and Francesco Scaresetti, bookends, Tra (1991), manufactured by Syn srl
IDEO Product Development, Paul Bradley and Lawrence Lam, computer pointing device, 3-D Mouse (1991), manufactured by Logitech Inc.
IBM Corporate Strategic Design, Richard Sapper and Samuel Lucente, computer Leapfrog (1989), manufactured by IBM Corporation
Per Jan of Pacesetter AB and Jan Ohrn of Utvecklingsdesign, pacemaker, Multilog 2040 (1988), manufactured by Pacesetter AB
Kirk Jones and Doug Olson, bicycle wheel, Spin™ (1989), manufactured by Innovations in Composites Inc.
Masayuki Kurokawa, pen, Gom (1992), manufactured by Fuso Gum Industry Co. Ltd
Masayuki Kurokawa, push pins and magnets, Gom (1984), manufactured by Fuso Gum Industry Co. Ltd
Ross Lovegrove of Studio X, Stephen Peart of Vent Design and Knoll in-house design team, lumbar support, Surf™ Collection (1994), manufactured by The Knoll Group
Hans Maier-Aichen, wastepaper baskets, LIP (1993), manufactured by Authentics artipresent GmbH
Enzo Mari, box, Flores (1991), manufactured by Danese srl
Jasper Morrison, storage module, Bottle (1993), manufactured by Magis srl
Marc Sadler, motorcyclist's back protector, Bap (1992), manufactured by Dainese SpA
Richard Sapper and Marco Zanuso, line radio receiver (1971), manufactured by Brionvega
Paul Schudel, wall clock, DK (1980), manufactured by Designum
Wayman R. Spence, UltraSoft® Blue Gel Comfort Pad (1994), manufactured by WRS Sportsmed
Vent Design, Stephen Peart and Bradford Bissell, wet suit, Animal (1988), manufactured by O'Neill Inc.

Philadelphia Museum of Art, Pennsylvania

Gordon Baldwin, earthenware, Dark Round Form (1996)
Emmanuel Cooper, stoneware, Jug (1996)
Emmanuel Cooper, stoneware, Jug (1997)
Philippe Starck, toilet brush, Excalibur (1995), manufactured by Heller Designs
Philippe Starck, DADADA stool, (1993), manufactured by XO
Philippe Starck, BUBU 1er stool (1991), manufactured by XO
Philippe Starck, lemon squeezer, Juicy Salif (1990–91), manufactured by Alessi SpA

Philippe Starck, colander, Max Le Chinois (1990–91), manufactured by Alessi SpA
Philippe Starck, creamer, Su Mi Tang (1992), manufactured by Alessi SpA
Philippe Starck, teapot, Ti Tang (1992), manufactured by Alessi SpA
Philippe Starck, chair, Costes (1984), manufactured by Driade SpA
Philippe Starck, table/chair, Lola Mundo (1988), manufactured by Driade SpA
Philippe Starck, chair, Boom Rang (1992), manufactured by Driade SpA
Philippe Starck, armchair, J. (Serie Lang) (1987), manufactured by Driade SpA
Philippe Starck, kettle, Hot Bertaa (1990–91), manufactured by Alessi SpA
Philippe Starck, floor lamp, Rosy Angelis (1994)

Acquisitions/Photographic Credits

The publisher and editors would like to thank the designers and manufacturers who submitted work for inclusion, and the following photographers and copyright holders for the use of their material (page numbers are given in parentheses):

Rike Baetcke (95 left) – Jan Bengtsson (64 right, 70 right) – Adolf Bereuter (47) – Fabrizio Bergamo (25) – Boym Design Studio (112 left) – J.F. Cantrel (99 left) – Bitetto Chimenti fotografia srl (44) – J.-P. Cochet (200 left) – Karen Collins (198) – Rick English (172–3) – Gino Gareza (52) – Michael Gerlach (39) – Lars Gundersen (145) – Doug Hall (208 right, 209) – Hans Hansen (6 left) – Julian Hawkins (62) – Anthony Hill (9) – Shinichi Kayama (178) – Stefan Kirchner (8 above left, right top and bottom) – Hisashi Kudoh (199) – Carlo Lavatori (211) – Richard Learoyd (169 right) – © Morgane Le Gall (114–17, 125, 126 right, 127, 158) – Marsel Loermans (108, 129 left) – Marco Melander (51 left) – P.J. Muner (180) – Andres Otero (75 right) – Alessandro Paderni (22) – Alexandre Peraud (17) – Mathias Pettersson (196 left) – Jan Pohribny (70 left) – Udo Pusch (109 centre) – Sergio Ebrem Raimondi (55 left) – M. Ramazzotti (20, 24 bottom, 63 left) – Markus Richter (210 left) – Sheila Rock (109 right) – Hidetoyo Sasaki (174–7) – Winfried Scheuer (82 left) – Schiebel Elektronische Geräte GmbH (192–3) – © Schnakenburg and Brahl fotografi (34) – SCP (169 left) – Luciano Soave (23, 50 left, 64 left, 197); Tom Stewart (18, 65 left) – Studio Diametro (32, 60) – Studio Frei (7 left) – Studio Rosenthal (113, 128) – Isao Takahashi (129 right) – Leo Torri (41, 79 left and right, 90–1, 132) – Jason Tozer (130) – Massimo Troboldi (82 right) – Tom Vack (67) – Peer van der Kruis (118) – Hans van der Mars (112 right, 121, 122) – Eugène van Veldhoven (164–5) – VIA/D. Ikentrenie (205) – Marco Vigano (123) – Gianluca Widmer (119) – Miro Zagnoli (7 bottom right, 79 centre) – Andrea Zani (92) – Patrick Zier (48)

Acierno ISL srl, Via Viperano 50, Palermo 90146, Italy. T: (0)91 513947/521168. F: (0)91 518287
Adatte Design, Chemin du Petit-Flon 25, Le Mont 1052, Switzerland. T: (0)21 643 10 50. F: (0)21 643 10 59
Aero, 46 Weir Road, Wimbledon, London SW19 8UG, UK. T: (0)181 971 0022. F: (0)181 971 0033
Agape srl, Via Ploner 2, Mantova 46038, Italy. T: (0)376 371738. F: (0)376 374213
Alessi SpA, Via Privata Alessi 6, Omegna 28026, Verbania VB, Italy. T: (0)323 868611. F: (0)323 866132
Alias srl, Via dei Videtti 2, Grumello del Monte 24064, Bergamo, Italy. T: (0)35 44 20 240. F: (0)35 44 20 996
AllGlass Snc, Via dell'Artigianato 16, Massanzago (Padua) 35010, Italy. T: (0)49 5797944. F: (0)49 5797091
Amano Shikki Co. Ltd, 245 Haoka, Takaoka City 933, Toyama, Japan. T: (0)766 23 2151. F: (0)766 25 6150
A1 Laboratory Supplies, 2A/4 Avery Hill Road, London SE9 2BD, UK. T: (0)181 850 0907. F: (0)181 859 6026
Apple Computer Inc., 20730 Valley Green Drive, Cupertino 95014, California, USA. T: (0)650 728 0530. F: (0)415 495 0251
Arcade, Via Goethe 2, Bolzano 39100, Italy. T: (0)471 980795. F: (0)471 977592
Artemide SpA, Via Bergamo 18, Pregnana Milanese (MI) 20010, Italy. T: (0)2 93518.1. F: (0)2 93518390
Asplund, 31 Sibyllegatan, Stockholm 11442, Sweden. T: (0)8 6625284. F: (0)8 6623885
Atelier srl, Via Monviso 52, Mariano Comense Como 22066, Italy. T: (0)31 743323. F: (0)31 746233
Les Ateliers du Nord, Place du Nord 2, Lausanne CH 1005, Switzerland. T: (0)21 320 58 07. F: (0)21 320 58 43
Authentics, Max-Eyth-Strasse 30, Holzgerlingen 71088, Germany. T: (0)7031 68 05 0. F: (0)7031 68 05 99
Avarte Oy, Hiekkakiventie 2, Helsinki FIN-00710, Finland. T: (0)9 350 80732. F: (0)9 350 80780
Shin and Tomoko Azumi, 953 Finchley Road, London NW11 7PE, UK. T/F: (0)181 731 7496

B&B Italia, Strada Provinciale 32, Novedrate (CO) 22060, Italy. T: (0)31 795111. F:(0)31 791592
Gijs Bakker, Keizersgracht 518, Amsterdam 1017 EK, The Netherlands. T: (0)20 6382986. F: (0)20 6388828
Baleri Italia, Via F. Cavallotti 8, Milan 20122, Italy. T: (0)2 76014672. F: (0)2 76014419
Boym Design Studio, 17 Little West 12 Street, No. 301A, New York, NY 10014, USA. T: (0)212 807 8210. F: (0)212 807 8211
Box Design AB, 17B Repslagereg, Stockholm 118 46, Sweden. T: (0)8 6401212. F: (0)8 6401216
BRF srl, Colle Val D'Elsa (Siena) 53034, Loc. S. Marziale, Italy. T: (0)577 929418. F: (0)577 929648
Debbie Jane Buchan, 3 Hutchison Avenue, Edinburgh EH14 1QE, Scotland. T: (0)131 539 9036
Bute Fabrics Ltd, Rothesay, Isle of Bute, PA20 0DP, Scotland. T: (0)1700 503734. F: (0)1700 504545

Campana Objetos Ltda, Rua Barão de Tatui 219, São Paulo 01226030, São Paulo, Brazil. T: (0)11 36664152. F: (0)11 8253408
Campeggi srl, Via del Cavolto 8, Anzano del Parco (Como) 22040, Italy. T: (0)31 630495. F: (0)31 632205
Cappellini SpA, Via Marconi 35, Arosio (CO) 22060, Italy. T: (0)31 759111. F: (0)31 763322/763333
Cassina SpA, Via Busnelli 1, Meda 20036, Milan, Italy. T: (0)362 3721. F: (0)362 342246
Ceramica Flaminia, S.S. Flaminia km 54,630, 01033 Civita Castellana (VT), Italy. T: (0)761 540245. F: (0)761 540069
ClassiCon GmbH, Perchtinger Strasse 8, Munich 81379, Germany. T: (0)89 74 81 33-0. F: (0)89 78 09 99 6
Colebrook Bosson Saunders Products Ltd, 18 Bowden Street, London SE11 4DS, UK. T: (0)171 587 5283. F: (0)171 587 5275
Comma Inc., 9 West 19th Street, 4th Floor, New York, NY 10011, USA. T: (0)212 929 4866. F: (0)212 924 3667
Covo srl, Via Salaria 741, Rome 00138, Italy. T: (0)6 88 64 10 95. F: (0)6 88 64 11 45

Paul Daly c/o Space PR, 214 Westbourne Grove, London W11 2RH, UK. T: (0)171 229 6533. F: (0)171 727 0134
Dd David Design, Stortorget 25, Malmö 21134, Sweden. T: (0)40 30 00 00. F: (0)40 30 00 50
M.W.G. de Laat, Schijndelseweg 116, Boxtel 5283 AG, The Netherlands
De Padova, Corso Venezia 14, Milan 20121, Italy. T: (0)2 76008413. F: (0)2 783201/76008675
Droog Design for Rosenthal, Keizersgracht 518, Amsterdam 1017 EK, The Netherlands. T: (0)20 6382986. F: (0)20 6388828
Drop Design, Roslagsgatan 37, 113 54 Stockholm, Sweden. T/F: (0)815 71 11

Edra Mazzei, PO Box 28, Perignano 56030, Italy. T: (0)587 616660. F: (0)587 617500
Epson, 3-3-5 Owa, Suwa-shi, Nagano 392-8502, Japan
Ezech Limited, 9/F Cheung Lung Ind. Bldg, 10 Cheung Yee Street, Cheung Sha Wan, Kowloon, Hong Kong. T: (0)852 2743 2511. F: (0)852 2371 3473

Fabbian Illuminazione SpA, Via Santa Brigida 50, Rosana, Treviso 31020, Italy. T: (0)423 784535. F: (0)423 484395
Roberto Feo, 26 Northfield House, Frensham Street, London SE15 6TL, UK. T: (0)171 732 6614. F: (0)171 277 6761
Fiskars Consumer Oy Ab, Billnäs FIN-10330, Finland. T: (0)19 277721. F: (0)19 236350
Flexform SpA, Via Einaudi 23/25, Meda, Milan 20036, Italy. T: (0)362 3991. F: (0)362 73055
Flos c/o Di Palma PR, Corso Venezia 37, Milan 20121, Italy. T: (0)2 76021515. F: (0)2 76009606

Klaus Hackl, Steinstrasse 79A, Munich 81667, Germany. T/F: (0)89 48953028
Hackman Designor Oy Ab, Hämeentie 135, Box 130, Helsinki FIN-00561, Finland. T: (0)204 39 11. F: (0)204 395 742
Masako Hayashibe, 3-11-31-315, Ikejiri, Setagaya, Tokyo 154-0001, Japan. T/F: (0)3 3412 8216
Heller Incorporated, 41 Madison Avenue, New York, NY 10010, USA. T: (0)212 685 4200. F: (0)212 685 4204

Idee Co. Ltd, 6-1-16, Minami Aoyama 1017, Minato-ku, Tokyo, Japan. T: (0)33409 7080. F: (0)3 3486 1580
IDEO Japan, 413 Axis Building, 5-17-1 Roppongi, Minato-ku, Tokyo 106, Japan. T: (0)3 5570 2664. F: (0)3 5570 2669
IKEA of Sweden, Box 702, Älmhult 343 81, Smaland, Sweden. T: (0)476 8100 00. F: (0)476 15123
Ikepod Watch Company AG, Alpenstrasse 14, PO Box 4534, CH-6304 Zug, Switzerland. T: (0)41 711 4727. F: (0)41 711 4728
Inflate, 5 Old Street, London EC1V 9HL, UK. T: (0)171 251 5453. F: (0)171 250 0311
Inredningsform/Iform, Davidshallsgatan 20, Malmö, Box 5055, SE-200 71, Sweden. T: (0)40 303610. F: (0)40 302288
Issey Miyake Inc., 45-14 Oyama-cho, 151 0065 Shibuya-ku, Tokyo, Japan. T: (0)3 5454 1705. F: (0)3 5454 1715

Kartell c/o Von Wedel Public Relations, Via G. Giusti 26, Milan 20154, Italy. T: (0)2 33104675. F: (0)2 33106747 or **Kartell SpA**, Via delle Industrie 1, Noviglio (Milan) 20082. T: (0)2 90012.1. F: (0)2 9053316
Koizumi Studio, 2F 2-2-34 Fujimidai, Kunitachi-City, 186-0003 Tokyo, Japan. T/F: (0)42 574 1458.
Kokusai Kako Co. Ltd, 4-11-17 Minami Senba, Chuo-ku 542, Ousaka-fu, Japan. T: (0)6 251 2931. F: (0)6 251 8830
Konsepti, 4 E. Krasnohorske, Prague 110 00, Czech Republic. T: (0)2 232 6928. F: (0)2 232 1358
Kusch & Co., Sitzmöbelwerke GmbH & Co. KG, Gundringhausen 5, D-59969 Hallenberg, Germany. T: (0)2984 300 0. F: (0)2984 300 177

Laboratorio Pesaro, Via della Produzione 94, Montelabbate 61025, Pesaro, Italy. T: (0)721 481188. F: (0)721 481454
Ligne Roset, b.p. No. 9 Briord 01470, France. T: (0)4 74 36 17 00. F: (0)4 74 36 16 95
Luceplan SpA, Via E.T. Moneta 46, Milan 20161, Italy. T: (0)2 66242.1 F: (0)2 66203400
Lush Lily, 123 South Park, San Francisco 94103, California, USA. T: (0)415 823 1163. F: (0)415 495 0251

Magis srl, Via Magnadola 15, Motta di Livenza (TV) 31045, Italy. T: (0)422 768742-3. F: (0)422 766395
Matsushita Electric Industrial Co. Ltd, Corporate Design Centre, 2-1-61, Shiromi, Chuo-ku 540-0001, Osaka, Japan. T: (0)6 949 2041. F: (0)6 947 5606
MDF Italia srl, Via Wittgens 3, Milan 20123, Italy. T: (0)2 58311300. F: (0)2 58311277/583135
Montina, Via Comunale del Rovere 13/15, San Giovanni al Natisone 33048, Udine, Italy. T: (0)432 756081. F: (0)432 756036
Montis, Steenstraat 2, Postbus 153, Dongen 5107 NE, The Netherlands. T: (0)31 162 377777. F: (0)31 162 377710
Nils Holger Moormann Möbel Produktions-und Handels GmbH, Kirchplatz, Aschau 83229, Germany. T: (0)8052 4001. F: (0)8052 4393
Moroso SpA, Via Nazionale 60, Cavalicco (Ud) I-33010, Italy. T: (0)432 577111. F: (0)432 570761
Murano Due, Via delle Industrie 16, 30030 Salzano, Venice, Italy. T: (0)41 5740292. F: (0)41 5744070

N2, 64 Breisacherstrasse, Basle 4057, Switzerland. T/F: (0)61 693 4015
NEC America/Packard Bell, 339 North Bernardo Avenue, Mountain View, California 94043-5223, USA. T: (0)650 528 5564
NEC Corporation, Corporate Design Division, 7-1 Shiba 5-Chome, Minato-ku, Tokyo 108-01, Japan
NEC Corporation – Plasma Display Business Promotion Division, Mita Kokusai Building, 4–28, Mita 1-chome, Minato-ku 108–0073, Tokyo, Japan. T: (0)3 3798 7273. F: (0)3 3798 7347
Néotù, 25 Rue du Renard, Paris 78004, France. T: (0)1 42 78 96 97. F: (0)1 42 78 26 27
Nuno Corporation, B1F Axis Bldg, 5-17-1 Roppongi, Minato-ku, Tokyo 106, Japan. T: (0)3 3586 9365. F: (0)3 3505 6206
Novikos International srl, Via Mure 109, Altivole (Treviso) 31030, Italy. T: (0)423 915077. F: (0)423 915027
Nya Nordiska, An den Ratswiesen, Dannenberg D-29451, Germany. T: (0)5861 8090. F: (0)5861 80912

Katsuhiko Ogino, 3-2-2, Shinjukuku, Shinjuku, Tokyo, Japan. T/F: (0)3 3358 4890
Oluce, Via Cavour 52, S. Giuliano Milanese, Milan, Italy. T: (0)2 98491435. F: (0)2 98490779
Olympus Optical Co. (Europa) GmbH, Wendenstrasse 14–16, Hamburg 20097, Germany. T: (0)40 237 73 0. F: (0)40 23 37 65/23 07 61

Pallucco Italia SpA, Via Azzi 36, Castagnole de Paese, Treviso 31040, Italy. T: (0)422 43 88 00
Verre Perrier, Cristallerie diArques, 41 Avenue du General de Gaulle, Arques 62510, France
Philips Lighting BV, Mr F.J. Haarmanweg 25, Terneuzen 4538 AN, The Netherlands. T: (0)115 684318. F: (0)115 684448
Posch Collection, Bergshäuser Strasse 15, Kassel 34123, Germany. T: (0)561 576097. F: (0)561 576090
Produzione Privata, Via Pallavicino 31, Milan 20145, Italy. T: (0)2 43008302. F: (0)2 43008222
Proto Design Lda, Rua da Vinha, Lisbon 43A 1200, Portugal. T: (0)1 342 8508. F: (0)1 342 0239
Punt Mobles SL, 48 Islas Baleares, Fuente del Jarro 46988, Valencia, Spain. T: (0)96 1320013. F: (0)96 1320287

RADI Designers, 89 Rue de Turenne, Paris 75003, France. T: (0)1 42 71 29 57. F: (0)1 42 71 29 62
Readymade, 147 W 26th Street 5FL, New York, NY 10001, USA. T: (0)212 726 2862. F: (0)212 989 9473
Rexite SpA, Via Edison 7, Cusago (Milan) 20090, Italy. T: (0)2 90390013. F: (0)2 90390018
Vibeke Rohland, 19 Holbergsgade, Copenhagen DK-1057K, Denmark
Roland Plastics Ltd, Wickham Market, Woodbridge, Suffolk IP13 0QZ, UK. T: (0)1728 747777. F: (0)1728 748222
Rosenthal AG, Wittelsbacherstrasse 43, Selb 95100, Germany. T: (0)9287 72566. F: (0)9287 72271

Rolf Sachs, 101 Farm Lane, Unit 3A, London SW6 1QY, UK. T: (0)171 610 0777. F: (0)171 386 9344
Sawaya & Moroni SpA, Via Andegari 18, Milan 20121, Italy. T: (0)2 863951. F: (0)2 86464831
Schiebel Elektronische Geräte GmbH, Margaretenstrasse 112, Vienna A-1050, Austria. T: (0)1 546260. F: (0)1 542339
Schmidinger Modul Wohn & Objektbedarf GmbH, Stangenach 146, Schwarzenberg A-6867, Vorarlberg, Austria. T: (0)5512 27 82 14. F: (0)5512 27822
SCP Limited, 135–139 Curtain Road, London EC2A 3BX, UK. T: (0)171 739 1869. F: (0)171 729 4224
Segis SpA, Via Umbria 14, Poggibonsi (Siena) 53036, Italy. T: (0)577 980333. F: (0)577 938090
Seiko Corporation Ltd, 15–1 Kyobashi, 2-chome, Chou-ku, Tokyo 104, Japan. T: (0)3 3563 9136. F: (0)3 3563 9591
Sharp Corporation, Corporate Design Centre, 22-22 Nagaike-cho, Abeno-ku, Osaka 545 8522, Japan. T: (0)6 621 3637 F: (0)6 629 1162
Michael Sodeau, 25D Highgate Westhill, London N6 6NP, UK. T/F: (0)181 341 2026
Sony Corporation/Creative (Design) Centre, 5-11-13 Kitashinagawa, Shinagawa-ku, Tokyo 141, Japan. T: (0)3 5448 6100 F: (0)3 5448 7823
Studio Orange – Rock Galpin, 70–72 Kingsland Road, London E2 8DP, UK. T: (0)171 684 9422. F: (0)171 684 9423
Studio Ilkka Suppanen, Pohjoisranta 8 E 104, Helsinki 00170, Finland. T: (0)50 564 1081. F: (0)9 622 3093

Gebrüder Thonet GmbH, Michael Thonet Strasse 1, Frankenberg D-35066, Germany. T: (0)6451 508 0. F: (0)6451 508 108
Timorous Beasties, 7 Craigend Place, Glasgow G13 2UN, Scotland. T: (0)141 959 3331. F: (0)141 959 8880
Tonelli srl, Via della Produzione 33/49, Montelabbate (PS) 61025, Italy. T: (0)721 481172. F: (0)721 481291

Maarten Van Severen, Galgenberg 25, Ghent 9000, Belgium. T: (0)9 225 29 55. F: (0)9 233 11 42
Eugène van Veldhoven, Dunne Bierkade 29, Den Haag 2512 BD, The Netherlands. T/F: (0)70 3655237
Venini SpA, Fondamenta Vetrai 50, Murano 30141, Italy. T: (0)41 739955. F: (0)41 739369
Bourse VIA, 29-33 Avenue Daumesnil, Paris 75012, France. T: (0)1 46 28 11 11. F: (0)1 46 28 13 13

Wanders Wonders, Van Diemenstraat 296, 1013 CR Amsterdam, The Netherlands. T: (0)20 4221339. F: (0)20 4227519
I. Wiendels, Jasmijnstraat 31, Utrecht 3551 SP, The Netherlands
WMF/21, Eberhardstrasse, Geislingen/Steige D-73309, Germany. T: (0)7331 251. F: (0)7331 45387
Wogg AG, Im Grund 16, CH-5405 Baden-Dättwil, Switzerland. T: (0)56 493 38 21. F: (0)56 493 40 87

Yamaha Corporation, 10–1 Nakazawa-cho, Hamamatsu, Shizuoka Prefecture 4308650, Japan. T: (0)53 460 2883. F: (0)53 463 4922
Yamakado, Viaduc des Arts, 65 Avenue Daumesnil, Paris F-75012, France. T: (0)1 43 40 79 79. F: (0)1 43 40 79 80

Zanotta SpA, Via Vittorio Veneto 57, Nova Milanese 20054, Milan, Italy. T: (0)362 368330. F: (0)362 451038

Suppliers